PARENTING A CHILD WITH ADHD

HOW TO PREPARE YOUR CHILD FOR SCHOOL LIFE, INTEGRATE EXECUTIVE FUNCTIONING SKILLS, AND FOSTER SUCCESSFUL FRIENDSHIPS

ROSE LYONS

© **Copyright 2022 - All rights reserved.**

The content contained within this book may not be reproduced, duplicated or transmitted without direct written permission from the author or the publisher.

Under no circumstances will any blame or legal responsibility be held against the publisher, or author, for any damages, reparation, or monetary loss due to the information contained within this book, either directly or indirectly.

Legal Notice:

This book is copyright protected. It is only for personal use. You cannot amend, distribute, sell, use, quote or paraphrase any part, or the content within this book, without the consent of the author or publisher.

Disclaimer Notice:

Please note the information contained within this document is for educational and entertainment purposes only. All effort has been executed to present accurate, up to date, reliable, complete information. No warranties of any kind are declared or implied. Readers acknowledge that the author is not engaged in the rendering of legal, financial, medical or professional advice. The content within this book has been derived from various sources. Please consult a licensed professional before attempting any techniques outlined in this book.

By reading this document, the reader agrees that under no circumstances is the author responsible for any losses, direct or indirect, that are incurred as a result of the use of the information contained within this document, including, but not limited to, errors, omissions, or inaccuracies.

CONTENTS

Introduction	7
1. ADHD—A CONDITION, NOT A CURSE	15
Understanding ADHD—The First Step to Becoming a Better Parent for Your Child	16
What Is ADHD?	17
The Three Types of ADHD and Their Symptoms	19
Common Signs of ADHD in Children	22
Symptoms in Multiple Settings	24
2. WHAT CAUSES ADHD AND WHAT DOESN'T	25
Some Possible Causes of ADHD	25
What Doesn't Cause ADHD - Debunking Some Common Myths and Fears	28
Environmental Factors	34
3. THE BIOLOGY OF ADHD AND NON-ADHD BRAIN	39
The ADHD vs. Non-ADHD Brain	40
How ADHD Is Diagnosed	46
4. TALKING TO YOUR CHILD ABOUT ADHD	55
Explaining ADHD to Your Child	56
Tips for Starting the Conversation	59
Talking About the Bright Side	62
Benefits of ADHD	64
Putting These Benefits to Good Use	68

5. SELF-CARE WHILE DEALING WITH
   ADHD CHILDREN — 71
   Effective Self-Care Tips for Parents of
   ADHD Children — 72
   Parenting Tips for Single Parents on
   Raising ADHD Children — 83
   Handling Marital Life — 87

6. PARENTING STRATEGIES FOR
   HELPING YOUR ADHD CHILD -
   AT HOME — 91
   Pro-Parenting Tips for Raising ADHD
   Children — 92
   What Parents Should not Do — 99
   Teaching Hygiene to Your ADHD child — 101

7. PARENTING STRATEGIES FOR
   HELPING YOUR ADHD CHILD - AT
   SCHOOL — 105
   Executive Function — 106
   Parenting Tips for Helping Your ADHD
   child at school — 115
   Helping Your Child With Their
   Homework — 123
   Strategies for ADHD Children at School — 128

8. ADHD MEDICATION AND
   TREATMENT — 135
   Meds On, Meds Off – When and When
   Not to Take Medication for ADHD — 135
   Tips for Stopping ADHD Medication and
   Minimizing Side Effects — 139
   Medication for Treating ADHD — 141
   Coping With Side Effects of ADHD
   Medication — 146
   Contacting the Doctor — 148
   Pharmacogenetic Testing — 149

9. NATURAL REMEDIES FOR TREATING
   ADHD 151
   Natural Strategies and Remedies for
   Treating ADHD 151
   Behavioral Therapy and ADHD 157
   Behavioral Therapy for Children
   With ADHD 159
   Behavioral Therapist - Why You Need
   One and How to Get One 160

10. SUPPORT RESOURCES FOR PARENTS ... 163
    Best ADHD Podcasts 164
    Best ADHD Apps 168

11. MAKING AND KEEPING FRIENDS 171
    Helping Your ADHD Child With Building
    Friendships 173
    Tips to Help You Prepare Your ADHD
    Child for a Playdate 178
    Explaining Your Child's ADHD Behavior
    to Other Parents 179

    Conclusion 183
    References 189

INTRODUCTION

One thing that hinders communication, especially between parents and their children, is a simple fact that no two people are alike. To illustrate this, think about the people (or person) in your life whom you believe are your opposites. As friends, family members, or colleagues, we all have people whose interests, personality traits, and perspectives sharply contrast with ours. Now, imagine being responsible for raising them as your children.

For parents raising children with Attention Deficit Hyperactivity Disorder (ADHD), this is more than just a visualization exercise; it is a daily reality. Children are typically poor communicators, and it is even more challenging to understand and help them when they also have ADHD.

The most apparent symptoms of this disorder are impulsivity, inattentiveness, and impatience. Unfortunately, since this behavior is not learned but is a result of nature, there is not much the affected child can do about the disorder to just stop the negative behaviors. Indeed, children are often unaware that they have a condition and that issues must be addressed.

Parents, however, are usually quite observant, and they can see that their child's behavior is not just problematic now but may also be derailing in the future. So before they put the pieces together, they may ask questions like, "Why doesn't he listen to me?"; "What do I do to make her sit still at the dinner table?"; "How am I failing my child?"

You are not alone in this worry. About 2.2% of children worldwide struggle with ADHD (ADDitude, 2022). In the United States alone, 6.1 million children have been diagnosed with the disorder (CDC, 2021). Nevertheless, it is essential to remember that your children are having a rough time too. As children grow older, they will notice the effect that their behavior has on other people, as well as on themselves. However, as mentioned before, children can do little or nothing about this condition unless they are helped by their parents (or any other type of guardian). What they need more than anything else is your love and support.

The fact that you are reading this book shows that you are heavily invested in your child's well-being. You want them to be successful in various areas of life, including socially and educationally. So it can easily be deduced that you are ready to learn how to make your child with ADHD comfortable and happy. This willingness to make the right choices for your child is an important step.

The first task this book undertakes is the correction of a common misconception that people have regarding ADHD. Although it is a disorder, it is not a life sentence. Your child who has the condition of this disorder is not destined for a failed future, and the first chapter of this book will show you why. How you perceive this condition will inform how you interact with your child and the measures you can take to help them.

Because of the problems associated with ADHD, many people are often quick to describe it as a curse. This sentiment may even be shared by adults diagnosed with the condition. Although this perception is erroneous, we should not be quick to dismiss it, as it may not be the result of malice or prejudice. In truth, ADHD *can* be hard to live with.

For one, success in any endeavor requires focused attention. Without this, your high IQ and talent may not count for much. One of the most common symptoms of ADHD is a seeming inability to keep one's mind focused on a single task for a meaningful length of time. People with this condition tend to be quickly and more frequently distracted than neurotypicals.

However, it should be noted that this distraction typically happens when the affected child has little interest in a particular task. Therefore, on those activities that they do not find boring, people with ADHD may become *hyper-focused* (Low, 2021).

If your child is also hyperactive, their behavior may be described as unruly and, at the worst, wild and disorderly. You can imagine the impact this could have on the sociability of your child and all the ways it may affect their emotional and mental development. As such, we should forgive those who declare ADHD a curse.

ADHD is merely a condition that can be managed. Indeed, your affected child has every chance to foster meaningful and long-term relationships. In addition, they can succeed at any task and become valuable members of society despite their ADHD.

Need proof? You may not know this, but several prominent figures, from politicians to scientists, have this condition.

James Carville is a political consultant who has been instrumental in helping politicians—both in the United States and other countries—secure public office. He is famously credited with Bill Clinton's 1992 presidential victory. In 2004, James Carville admitted on CNN that he had ADHD. This condition caused him to drop out of college, but he eventually graduated from law school and found his passion for politics.

How about the Pulitzer prize winner, Katherine Ellison? Although she was not diagnosed with the condition until 2007, when she was 49 years old, Katherine has distinguished herself as an author and journalist.

Sir Richard Branson is another notable figure who has achieved significant and admirable things. You may know him as the founder of the world-class airline Virgin Atlantic. However, did you also know that he has been diagnosed with ADHD and dyslexia? It presented some problems for him, as he recounts struggling in school and being unable to focus on things he did not have a passion for.

However, Sir Richard has used this condition to his advantage. Hyper-focus, which may result from having ADHD, helped grow his business into its current conglomerate. Since people with ADHD have a 300% likelihood of starting a business, we may conclude that this condition compelled Branson to found his first business at age 16.

There are many other famous names whose exploits disprove the notion that ADHD is a curse. The founder of IKEA, Ingvar Kamprad, and superstar musician, Justin Timberlake are a couple of other examples.

This book, **Parenting a Child with ADHD**, has been painstakingly researched to equip you with the knowledge to help your child achieve their dreams while managing their ADHD. This book is 15 years in the making and is the product of personal experience and professional study.

Rose Lyons, the author of this book, has two lovely children, both of whom were diagnosed with Attention Deficit Hyperactivity Disorder. Her journey in helping her children has provided her with first-hand knowledge on how to deal with the condition. Rose has also carried out several studies on not just ADHD but other mental health conditions. She has gone on to help other parents successfully confront and overcome the challenges posed by ADHD. She hopes to make even more people aware of the mental health needs of children and adults.

Before now, parents dismissed the symptoms of ADHD as nothing more than childish exuberance or laziness in the case of an inability to focus. Nevertheless, of course, parenting is by no means an easy job. It definitely can be challenging in both standard and unique ways. For Rose, the position of parenting is the most delicate and important one in the world, and she wants to help everyone become more successful at it. This book is an extension of her compassion toward every parent who struggles with the challenges of ADHD.

This book will give you the tools you need to create a supportive and nurturing environment for your children with ADHD. Regardless of their diagnosis, you can raise them to be independent and confident.

Prepare to discover more about Attention Deficit Hyperactivity Disorder than you had grasped previously. Prepare to learn about the structure and processes of the ADHD brain and how it differs from a neurotypical one. After reading this book, you will be able to interact more effectively with your child who has this condition. In addition, your parenting strategies will be fine-tuned to accommodate your child with ADHD. You will also learn about modern and effective treatments and medication to manage the condition.

Prepare to become the best possible parent for your child and their number one cheerleader.

1

ADHD — A CONDITION, NOT A CURSE

Meet Christie, a young child in elementary school. She has always been quite different from her peers but in a good way. She is funny, full of life, and brilliant. She is a curious child and loves to learn new things. She is one of the smartest and kindest children in her class. However, there is a flip side to her. She is sweet as sugar one minute, and she can be sour like salt candy the next. She has a temper problem, and even the tiniest things—like someone talking loudly or when she does not get to choose her cereals for breakfast—can set her off. As a result, her mother often has difficulty making her sit through their meals together. Christie is a mess at church, too, as she keeps pushing the other children in her pew.
She was even ousted from her class a few weeks ago

for misbehaving and has become the black sheep. Lately, Christie has been having issues sitting straight and focusing on lessons. Her mother does not want her to get on meds, fearing it will turn her baby girl into an addict.

Confused and frustrated, Christie's mother has come to a dead end. She does not know why her more than capable daughter exhibits odd behavior and struggles with specific tasks. She feels like a bad parent when she has to scold her daughter for wiggling too much, talking excessively, and being so forgetful, even when she is a good child.

UNDERSTANDING ADHD – THE FIRST STEP TO BECOMING A BETTER PARENT FOR YOUR CHILD

Does the above scenario sound familiar to you? Do you feel like you are the one in the story? Do you feel like you are at your wit's end with your child and nothing seems to help?

Chances are, you have not been able to get help or find a solution for your child because you have no idea what is wrong with them. On the one hand, they are perfectly healthy, and you do not see any physical or health challenges with them. But, on the other hand, if your child is anything like Christie, they struggle with a condition known as ADHD.

So, no, they are not just misbehaving because they want to. All the unpleasant attitudes which you notice are a result of ADHD. This can be worrisome, especially if you have no idea what this condition means. Raising children, in general, is a difficult task, but raising a child with ADHD can be an unimaginable challenge. The journey of caring for children with ADHD from childhood to adulthood is rough, punctuated by bouts of success and even more significant failures. It is a challenge that you need to take up fully armed with information.

WHAT IS ADHD?

Demystifying ADHD is the first step for you as a parent in understanding the condition.

So, what is it?

ADHD is an acronym for Attention Deficit Hyperactivity Disorder (ADHD). It is a mental health condition that induces varying hyperactivity and impulsive behaviors. The inability to focus on a particular task or sit still for a long time is a characteristic of a person with ADHD.

People with ADHD are inattentive and suffer fluctuations in their energy levels more often and at more severe rates than those who do not have the condition. The effect of this can usually be noticed in their home, school, and social life.

Past researchers used to refer to the symptoms that cause this condition as Attention Deficit Disorder (ADD). The term ADD has been outdated since 1987. The third edition of the Diagnostic and Statistical Manual of Mental Disorders (DSM-3) used to categorize the condition into two subtypes:

- ADD with hyperactivity
- ADD without hyperactivity

However, after a revision by the American psychiatric association, the two subtypes were merged to become ADHD. ADHD has joined the league of common childhood mental health conditions and is reported to affect around 9.4% of children and adolescents in the United States.

ADHD is a neurodevelopmental disorder that presents early in childhood. Although the average age of onset is usually seven years, diagnosis often comes later, during their teens. Children with ADHD have problems controlling spontaneous responses ranging from movement to attentiveness to speech.

ADHD is not a learning disability, although the symptoms can increase difficulty in learning. There is also a chance for children who have ADHD to have other disabilities such as dyslexia, anxiety, and ODD (Oppositional Defiance Disorder). Even though it is not a learning disability, its effects can still be lifelong.

THE THREE TYPES OF ADHD AND THEIR SYMPTOMS

ADHD is grouped into three types, namely:

- Inattentive type
- Hyperactive, impulsive type
- Combined type

The Inattentive Type

The inattentive type of ADHD borders on inattentiveness. Children with this type of ADHD struggle with focus, task completion, and keeping to instructions. Most researchers believe that children with this type of ADHD may go undiagnosed for a long time or receive improper diagnoses because they do not disturb the classroom. Girls who have ADHD often present with the inattentive type.

Symptoms of the Inattentive Type of ADHD

Children who struggle with the inattentive type of ADHD have the following symptoms:

- Frequent loss of items like books, homework, toys, and clothing
- Easily distracted by little occurrences in their surroundings
- Prone to making mistakes or missing details during study or work
- Difficulty maintaining focus when reading, listening, or having a conversation
- Have trouble paying attention when spoken to

The Hyperactive-Impulsive Type

This type of ADHD manifests as hyperactive and impulsive behaviors like:

- Fidgeting
- Interrupting others when they talk
- Impatience in waiting for their turn

The primary symptoms of this type of ADHD are:

- Excessive talking
- Difficulty playing or doing tasks quietly
- Difficulty sitting still
- Interrupting others when they are talking, playing, or doing other tasks
- Acting without thinking
- Difficulty controlling powerful emotions like anger and often having outbursts and temper tantrums
- Moving around constantly, like running and climbing inappropriately

The Combined Type

This type of ADHD is quite common. Children and even adults who experience this type display conditions of inattentive and hyperactive symptoms. Children often have difficulty paying attention, display impulsiveness, and have unusually high energy levels. A child with this type of ADHD presents mixed symptoms of the other types of ADHD.

Children with ADHD have a more challenging time fitting in than other children. This causes individual problems as well as stress on the family. It is common for parents who have no idea what ADHD is, or do not know how to solve their child's difficulties, to brand it a curse. However, no, ADHD is not a curse. It is just a childhood mental disorder that is manageable. If your child has ADHD, it does not mean they are troubled with an affliction or something metaphysical about their condition.

COMMON SIGNS OF ADHD IN CHILDREN

Regardless of the type of ADHD present in a child, these are the signs that can notify you to take action:

- **Self-focused behavior:** When a child cannot recognize the desires and needs of other people, it could be a sign that they have ADHD. This often progresses to symptoms like interrupting and difficulty waiting their turn.
- **Emotional troubles:** Children with ADHD have difficulty managing their emotions. It is common to find them bursting out in anger at odd times. If they are very young, they may display tantrums.
- **Fidgeting:** If a child has ADHD, they can hardly sit still. When asked to sit, they try to stand up, run around, fidget, or squirm.

- **Problems playing quietly:** Because they are often fidgety, it is difficult for children with ADHD to engage in quiet or calm play.
- **Unfinished tasks:** One of the significant signs of ADHD is leaving tasks unfinished. Children with ADHD often indicate interest in many things but cannot finish them. For instance, they begin projects, homework, or chores, but soon enough, they do something else that has caught their fancy.
- **Lack of focus:** A child with ADHD struggles with paying attention even when they are being addressed directly. After talking to them, they will admit they heard everything but cannot repeat what you said. Often, they hear your words but are unable to process them.
- **Avoidance of tasks needing extended mental effort:** Children with ADHD have difficulty focusing, which affects how they participate in activities that need comprehensive mental effort. These children often avoid mentally tasking activities, like doing homework or paying attention in class.
- **Mistakes:** One common sign of a child with ADHD is being mistake-prone. As they mainly have trouble heeding instructions that involve planning or plan execution, they often make

careless mistakes. However, this is not a sign of laziness or unintelligence.

- **Daydreaming:** Although people link noisiness and hyperactivity to children with ADHD, being quieter or more withdrawn than other children can be a sign of ADHD. More often than not, children with ADHD stare into space, daydream, and ignore the things around them.
- **The trouble with organization:** Children with ADHD cannot keep track of their tasks and activities. In school, this makes them get into trouble as they cannot make their homework, school projects, or other assignments a priority. This can make daily routines like getting ready seem like Groundhog's day at home.

SYMPTOMS IN MULTIPLE SETTINGS

When a child has ADHD, the symptoms manifest in different settings. The inattentiveness or hyperactive behavior will be noticed both at home and school.

2

WHAT CAUSES ADHD AND WHAT DOESN'T

ADHD is a common mental condition that is largely misunderstood, which is why scientists are trying to understand why it happens.

Since its first diagnosis and discussions, there have been different theories about why people have ADHD. However, there is no concrete proof of the exact cause of ADHD. Instead, scientists studying it for decades have highlighted some factors that potentially lead to its onset.

SOME POSSIBLE CAUSES OF ADHD

According to the Centers for Disease Control and Prevention (CDC) reports, around 9.4% of children in the United States have ADHD. Still, no scientist has pinpointed the exact cause of this condition. However, it is believed that some factors play a significant role in getting this condition. Some of these essential factors that influence ADHD are listed below:

Genes

Much research has revealed strong evidence linking genes to the development of ADHD. In addition, scientists' research indicates that this condition runs in families. People with close relatives with this condition are likely to have it, and individuals whose parents have the disorder are more likely to have it. However, the same genes that trigger the disorder are yet to be discovered. Ongoing research seeks to study the potential connection between the DRD4 gene and ADHD (Tovo-Rodrigues, et al., 2013). DRD4, also known as the dopamine receptor gene, is responsible for regulating the behaviors affected by the feel-good neurotransmitter dopamine. One typical example is risk-taking. Prior research in 1998 showed that this gene influences the brain's dopamine receptors (Swanson, et al., 1998).

Different gene variations have been observed in people with the disorder, making researchers believe that it is somewhat linked to the development of the condition. Chances are, there are several genes responsible for the condition. Even though genes play a role in the development of ADHD, people with no family history of the disorder have also been diagnosed with the condition. This disorder also depends on other factors, including a person's environment.

Neurotoxins

Some scientists say ADHD can be linked to common neurotoxic chemicals like lead and pesticides. In addition, pesticides containing organophosphates have also been connected to ADHD. Usually, these chemical pesticides are sprinkled on lawns and agricultural products, and children come in contact with them during play or through their food.

Studies have shown that organophosphates negatively affect the neurodevelopment of children.

Nutrition

Although there is speculation that food dyes and preservatives are responsible for causing hyperactivity in children, there is no strong evidence backing it. For example, many processed and packaged snack food ingredients include artificial coloring. In addition, edibles like jams, soft drinks, relishes, and food pies contain sodium benzoate for preservation. Again, however, there is no concrete evidence linking these food ingredients to ADHD.

Smoking and Alcohol

The environmental connection to ADHD in children happens before they are born. For example, pregnancy-related smoking is linked to specific ADHD symptoms in children. In addition, studies have shown that exposing children in the womb to alcohol and drugs increases their chances of having ADHD.

WHAT DOESN'T CAUSE ADHD - DEBUNKING SOME COMMON MYTHS AND FEARS

People think differently when they hear about ADHD, and the lack of understanding of ADHD negatively impacts the treatment of ADHD. In addition, widespread misinformation and myths about ADHD affect the individual's reaction to the condition. Therefore, these myths need to be clear, as they harm the ADHD community and prevent people from seeking diagnosis and treatment.

As such, people need to understand that the following do not cause ADHD:

- **Consuming sugar in excess:** Currently, no verifiable scientific evidence indicates that excess consumption of sugar in children causes ADHD. People often think eating sugar makes

children hyperactive, but it does not happen. Studies have not been able to link the two. Even though some studies suggest that children with ADHD can be sensitive to some food substances, there is no solid evidence to back it up.
- **Watching TV:** TV is often given a bad rep for its role in many child developmental problems and some ADHD symptoms. However, it does not directly cause ADHD. One of the main symptoms of ADHD is attention deficiency, and there is proof that watching too much TV reduces attention span. Looking at fast motion pictures for a long time over-stimulates the neurons connected with sound and sight. When these neurons are overstimulated, the neural centers do not respond well to ordinary stimulants.

As a result, concentrating on essential things requires more effort and time. Based on studies, children between the ages of one and three who are exposed to TV can have a reduced attention period by the time they are seven. However, the effects are not harmful enough to develop ADHD.

Some researchers maintain that the effects of TV on ADHD are inconclusive. Anybody who watches too much TV will struggle with attention deficiency, which is not limited to children without ADHD. Studies have also shown that the TV-watching habits of children with ADHD are the same as those without it (McBee, 2021). Many children worldwide watch TV most of the time, but they have never received an ADHD diagnosis. Meanwhile, ADHD has been diagnosed in children who do not have much access to the TV. Even though watching TV does not cause ADHD, parents must regulate how much time children spend watching TV.

- **Playing video games:** Some people think that letting their children play video games can make them have ADHD. The rationale is baseless, as no evidence indicates that playing video games causes ADHD. Like with TV, children and adults who spend more time looking at the screen struggle to maintain attention than others, but that does not lead to ADHD. Researchers suggest that children cannot get ADHD just by spending too much time behind the screen.
- **Poor parenting:** When a child has been diagnosed with ADHD, many parents carry the guilt upon themselves. Their guilt is often borne out of wishing that there was something they could do to make their children manage

their symptoms. The myth of ADHD resulting from poor parenting is why most parents think their child's diagnosis is their fault.

While a person with ADHD benefits from structure, more harm is done in the long run if they are repeatedly punished for symptoms like hyperactivity, restlessness, or impulsivity. However, these ADHD behaviors are often seen as poor manners, and the parents receive the blame for not controlling their child.

Girls Do Not Get ADHD

Usually, young girls are not hyperactive like young boys. Therefore, people rarely detect ADHD in girls because females do not display as many behavioral problems as males. This reduces the chance of referring girls for ADHD evaluation.

As a result of this myth, more girls live with untreated ADHD, which worsens and makes them have issues like:

- Mood
- Anxiety
- Antisocial personality
- Other comorbid disorders in adulthood

Girls *can* be diagnosed with ADHD, and it is just as important to identify their symptoms and provide them with the needed support.

People With ADHD Are Lazy

People who do not understand ADHD think of those individuals with the condition as lazy. As a result, a person with ADHD often feels guilty for being less productive and motivated due to this myth. Generally, people with ADHD require more structure and reminders to make things work, especially if they have to participate in activities requiring extended mental effort.

However, the myth about ADHD being a form of laziness is fueled by some symptoms, which manifest as disorganization, lack of interest, and motivation, with exceptions for activities the ADHD individual truly enjoys.

The truth is that people with ADHD love to accomplish things, but the struggle needed to complete seemingly simple tasks makes people regard them as lazy. They could be overwhelmed by doing things like cleaning their room. Myths like this should be discarded, as they make people feel like they have failed, eventually dropping their self-esteem.

Having ADHD Is **Not** *That Serious*

ADHD should be taken seriously, and parents should seek to understand the condition. The condition affects the individual's quality of life. Unlike others, people with ADHD have more chances of suffering from anxiety, mood, and substance use disorders.

Later in life, people with ADHD struggle with meeting work responsibilities and are often monitored or on probation. As a result, they are regularly afraid of losing their jobs and being less capable of fulfilling their financial needs, which can affect their personal life. In addition, although they require more time to complete tasks, educational and employment settings might not accommodate them.

ADHD Is Not a Real Medical Disorder

Some people see ADHD as a fad, but it is as real as it gets. Research shows visible differences between a brain with ADHD and one without it, including how they react with brain chemicals like dopamine, glutamate, and norepinephrine.

The brain sections linked with ADHD are crucial for executive functions, like:

- Planning
- Organizing

- Initiating tasks

ENVIRONMENTAL FACTORS

Parents are often worried when their child is diagnosed with ADHD, as they try to figure out if it is a nature or nurture thing. Some parents begin to feel it is something in them or something they have done that's responsible. These feelings are usually stronger when one parent has the condition, and their child is diagnosed with it.

However, psychologists state that people with neurodevelopmental disorders have neurological differences that they are born with. So people are born with the condition, which does not just start as they grow. Quite a lot of factors contribute to the onset of ADHD, but the impact of the environment plays a huge role.

Some psychologists assert that strong evidence links some environmental risk factors to a future ADHD diagnosis. Some of the environmental factors likely to cause ADHD include:

- In utero exposure
- Exposure to environmental toxins
- Illnesses

In Utero Exposure

According to relevant studies, when a pregnant woman smokes tobacco or drinks alcohol, there is a high chance that the child will eventually have ADHD. In addition, studies have shown that the risk of children having ADHD increases if their mothers are heavy smokers or if they drink more than four alcoholic drinks in one sitting.

Another in utero factor is the maternal diet, infections during pregnancy, and medications used, like caffeine, antidepressants, and antihypertensives. In addition, the American Psychiatric Association suggests the likelihood of developing ADHD increases in babies born early or at low birth weight.

Exposure to Environmental Toxins

Toxin exposure can play a significant role in utero or during childhood. Some toxins are lead, mercury, pesticides, and certain chemical compounds. For example, lead and pesticide organophosphate, which are found in the environment, can affect neurological development in children.

Illness

Some studies indicate that bacterial meningitis, a severe bacterial illness, can pose a risk for ADHD. Bacterial meningitis is transmitted through human-to-human contact and food, making it an environmental hazard. Another illness that places people at risk of ADHD is encephalitis, an inflammation in the brain caused by infection or autoimmune response.

The reality of ADHD, again, is that researchers have not been able to figure out the exact cause of it. Furthermore, this is likely because ADHD is not caused by just one thing. So it is difficult to pin down the cause to just one factor.

However, based on twin and family studies, genetics seems to be one of the significant factors. Unfortunately, though, genetic predisposition is not a surety that someone will have ADHD because of its many other risk factors. Often, ADHD is not caused by just one risk factor but is primarily a combination of genetic and environmental factors, which generally raises the chances of a person having the condition.

Psychologists admit that it is difficult to separate genetic and environmental factors because family members share genetics and lifestyle. Therefore, it is essential to consider all the predisposing factors since ADHD is the outcome of the total of those factors.

Other factors like brain damage have been seen to play a role in developing ADHD. For example, some ADHD diagnoses are often triggered by damage from head trauma, early life injuries, and atypical brain development.

Managing Environmental Stressors

ADHD is a neurodevelopmental condition caused mainly by genetics and environmental factors. Prevention of this condition is futile due to the genetic predisposition aspect of it. However, parents can manage the effect of environmental stressors on the health of their unborn children by taking steps like:

- Getting adequate prenatal healthcare
- Cutting off drug, alcohol, and tobacco exposure during pregnancy
- Reducing contact with environmental toxins like lead and pesticides

Most importantly, as a parent, you must understand that ADHD results from many factors. The debate about the exact cause is still ongoing, meaning you do not have to beat yourself up about your child's condition. There is no way you or anybody else could have prevented it, as there is no definite cause.

Some scientists argue that ADHD has no external cause, and people who have it are born with it, and it just escalates depending on time and their living conditions. Many theories have come up in the past years to explain the condition, but the truth remains that no one has been able to figure out an exact cause yet.

3

THE BIOLOGY OF ADHD AND NON-ADHD BRAIN

ADHD is a confusing and frustrating mental condition that takes a toll on the minds of the people living with it. In addition, they have to deal with an inconsistent way of living, as some days are good while others are shady.

As discussed earlier, scientists have spent their lives researching this condition and have listed dozens of telltale signs of the condition, yet they have not been successful in finding the root cause of it. However, discovering some crucial factors that play a role in aggravating ADHD is the closest anybody has ever come to profiling it.

As science has advanced with time, researchers and medical examiners have found some data on ADHD and its impairments to find a direction to do something about it. One such key study includes the study of the nervous system, explaining the differences between the ADHD brain and the brain without the condition.

THE ADHD VS. NON-ADHD BRAIN

ADHD is an actual condition. Despite what critics say about it, it exists, and there is enough data and real-life stories to support it. Unfortunately, cynics downplay or question its existence by blaming the symptoms on bad parenting or a lack of willpower and motivation from the individual with the condition, which is untrue. These dismissals of what is a real experience can be demoralizing for people with ADHD or their families.

However, people with ADHD can validate their experiences through the research results showing that stark differences exist between the ADHD brain and the non-ADHD brain. The brain of an individual with ADHD has a different structure, chemistry, and function than the normal's.

Brain Structure

The brain structures of people without ADHD have differences that affect many areas of the brain, which link to common ADHD symptoms.

Children with ADHD have noticeably smaller brains than those without. The difference in size can be seen in different brain regions like the amygdala and hippocampus, which connect emotion regulation, memory, and motivation. First, however, you need to know that the brain size difference does not play any role in their intelligence.

The National Institute of Health published a paper in 2007 stating that brain maturity is delayed in certain areas for a child with ADHD. The most notable delay point was the front of the cortex, which manages attention, and cognitive and planning control. The only region in the brain of an ADHD child with a maturation rate that's faster than average is the motor cortex, which connects to symptoms like fidgeting and restlessness.

Some regions in the frontal lobe of children with ADHD mature slower. Furthermore, since the frontal lobe is in charge of skills like attention, social behavior, and impulse control, children with ADHD may struggle with dysfunction associated with these skills. Regular activity in the frontal lobe's premotor and prefrontal cortex regions ensures motor activity and attentional capacity. Still, a person with ADHD has less activity in these brain regions.

The differences between a brain with ADHD and one without are more pronounced in children than adults.

Brain Function

The effect of ADHD on brain functioning is observed in different aspects. ADHD is connected to problems with cognitive, motivational, and behavioral functioning. It destabilizes mood regulation, emotions, and connections within the brain cells. It even disrupts how the brain communicates with its different parts.

The neurons in the brain are a network of nerve cells transporting information from one part of the brain to another. The neurons of people with ADHD develop slower and are not so efficient in sending some messages, bits of information, or behaviors. As a result of the slow development, the neurons may function abnormally in areas like a reward, focus, and movement.

Scientists use MRI and X-ray-based imaging tools to observe slight abnormalities in the brain function and structure of people with ADHD. Results from imaging of people with ADHD show that structural connectivity of the neurons is abnormal. However, the functional connectivity of people with ADHD is increased in some regions.

According to research based on comparisons with brains of people without this disorder, ADHD brains are hyperactive in some regions and hypoactive in others. The implication is that there could be a problem with the brain's computing ability to match cognitive demands adequately.

For instance, people with this condition find it difficult to manage brain activity in the regular attention network, causing distractions.

ADHD causes improper executive functioning skills in areas like:

- Attention
- Focus
- Concentration
- Memory
- Hyperactivity
- Impulsivity
- Social skills
- Organization
- Planning
- Decision making
- Task switching
- Learning from past mistakes
- Motivation

Some of the brain imaging techniques used to observe the functions of the ADHD brain include:

- Functional magnetic resonance imaging (fMRI)
- Positron emission tomography (PET)
- Single photon emission computed tomography (SPECT)

The brains of people with this condition have abnormalities in blood flow to certain parts of their brains, affecting the region's activity. In addition, children with this condition have different connectivities between the frontal cortex of the brain and the visual processing area. Studies and brain imaging techniques show that the ADHD brain does not process information similarly to a non-ADHD brain.

Brain Chemistry

The brain neurons transfer messages across the brain, and there is a gap between neurons, known as synapses. Synapses have to contain neurotransmitters for messages to be transmitted in the brain. Each neurotransmitter or chemical messenger has a unique function assigned to it.

Dopamine and noradrenaline are the major neurotransmitters. However, the brain of an ADHD person cannot properly regulate the dopamine system. For instance, the dopamine level is either too little, lacks receptors, or is not appropriately utilized. In the ADHD brain, having a high level of dopamine transporters without corresponding levels of receptors causes the brain to ignore important messages. This implies that dopamine travels too fast for the messages in the brain to be acknowledged.

The relevance of dopamine lies in managing the brain's reward and pleasure center and the sustenance of motivation and attention. Dopamine triggers children to determine the reward for a task. When a child perceives a reward as important, the dopamine levels spike, and the child takes up the task immediately.

Due to the abnormal dopamine functioning in the ADHD brain, there is little interest in routine tasks with low reward potential. As a result, the child with this disorder finds it difficult to start tasks or continue without distraction, making them lose interest in activities and move on to the next best thing.

An abnormal dopamine system enhances the difficulty for children in waiting for the things they want or taking action to get the reward in the future. It is difficult for them to picture future pleasure; they can only focus on things that have their attention *now*. Dopamine is great for learning, too. Activities that trigger high levels of dopamine in the brain are enjoyable, as the brain changes to recognize it, and the child finds it easier to repeat the behavior in the future.

HOW ADHD IS DIAGNOSED

The diagnosis for this condition is not made through objective tests like a blood test, physical test, or an X-ray. Only qualified doctors, psychiatrists, and psychologists can diagnose this condition using complete evaluation processes like:

- A comprehensive interview with the patient
- A review of medical history and school reports
- Attention, memory, and distractibility measurement tests

The information retrieved from the tests will then be compared with the Diagnostic and Statistical Manual of Mental Disorders (DSM) guideline for diagnosing this disorder. Although PET and fMRI are relevant for research, they cannot be used for diagnosis because they only determine the brain function during the period the test is taken. Brain scans cannot provide information for brain function in diverse situations like a clinical test. Again, scan data is usually based on group averages and does not apply to individuals.

Diagnostic Criteria

When a clinical test is done, the individual has to meet different conditions to get an official diagnosis. This applies to all types of ADHD; inattentive, hyperactive-impulsive, or combined. These are the conditions:

- Patient symptoms must be present before they turn twelve
- Patient symptoms must show up in multiple settings (home, school, work)
- Patient symptoms must interfere with daily activities
- Other mental health issues must not explain away a patient's symptoms

The diagnostic criteria for the three types of ADHD are described below:

Inattentive Type

When diagnosing children with the inattentive type of the disorder, a certain number of symptoms have to be recognized. Six or more symptoms of inattention must be seen in children 16 years old and under, while five or more symptoms need to be present in those 17 and older. In addition, the symptoms must have been observed for a minimum of six months before the test to receive a diagnosis for this condition.

An individual who is to be diagnosed with the inattentive type of ADHD needs to have some or all of these symptoms:

- Regularly making careless mistakes or ignoring details
- Has problems remaining focused on specific tasks or activities
- Hardly listening when spoken to
- Never finishing tasks or heeding instructions
- Problems with organization
- Has deep hatred for long-term tasks
- Regularly misplacing important items
- Very forgetful and easily distracted

Hyperactive-Impulsive Type

The age-based criteria for determining the hyperactive-impulsive type of ADHD is the same as the attentive, but based on the specific symptoms for the hyperactive-impulsive type of ADHD, which are:

- Constant fidgeting and squirming
- Continuous movement or restlessness in inappropriate places
- Inability to remain seated or stay in one spot
- Excessive talking
- Cannot remain quiet during leisure activities

- Has problems waiting their turn
- Responds before a question is finished being asked
- Regular interruption into other's conversation

Diagnosing a person with this condition is not the last stop. First, the health professional has to determine how severe it is by using this criterion:

1. Mild: The individual shows minor impairment in functioning but has enough symptoms to reach the diagnosis criteria
2. Moderate: The impairment is more pronounced
3. Severe: More than the minimum number of symptoms for diagnosis are present, as well as major impairment from the symptoms

Why Is an Accurate Diagnosis Important?

Due to the myths surrounding this condition, some parents might not be open to getting an official diagnosis for their children. Some are not interested in pursuing the potential medication needed, and others are worried about the stigma attached to having this disorder. However, getting an ADHD diagnosis is advantageous, and parents must shun hearsay if they suspect their children have the condition. Receiving an accurate diagnosis for this disorder boosts your chances of getting help, even if you do not show interest in using the medication as a treatment method.

Besides the apparent reason that a diagnosis is the first step to getting treatment, there are subtler benefits. It benefits you and your child emotionally because now you can put a name to the symptoms which your child has been presenting. ADHD symptoms can cause shame, embarrassment, and guilt. Most parents blame themselves and worry about their child's underperformance. It is natural for you or the child to get frustrated over the long periods it takes them to finish their tasks. Having a diagnosis keeps those emotions in check and keeps you from throwing the blame around.

Moreover, having written evidence of an official diagnosis can help get accommodations for the child with ADHD at school or in the workplace. Diagnosis for this condition is followed by a treatment course that enables you to manage the symptoms better.

Professionals Who Diagnose ADHD

Professionals qualified to diagnose this disorder include psychiatrists, psychotherapists, psychologists, neurologists, and some physicians. However, do not book an appointment with a health care provider until you find out if they have experience diagnosing this disorder.

If you do not know where to start with the assessments, discuss this with your family doctor so they can refer you to a qualified health care provider to do the assessments. Sometimes, pediatricians and general practitioners diagnose this condition, and when they suspect your child has it, they might provide you with a reference to see a specialist for extensive assessments.

Attempting to diagnose ADHD online is not ideal. While some quizzes and questionnaires online can be great as a self-screening process, they cannot act as an official diagnosis. The quiz, however, might be the force that propels you to reach out to a qualified medical examiner for that official diagnosis.

What to Share With Your Doctor or Medical Examiner

When diagnosing this condition, provide the doctor copies of relevant medical, school, or employment records. In addition, remember that you must provide a comprehensive family and social history. Some examiners send out questionnaires that will be completed before the appointment, so you must ensure that you present them at the appointment. Although a parent's consent is often needed before it is done, children's teachers or daycare providers sometimes get a copy of the questionnaires.

The Assessment Process

The duration of an ADHD assessment is dependent on the health care provider, but on average, it lasts for three hours. The methods are specific to the practitioners, but an in-person interview is inevitable. The topics discussed during the consultation include family, health, development, and lifestyle history.

Depending on the initial findings, the clinician may ask to interview other people who are closely related to the subject. For example, the clinician might request to speak with a teacher, daycare provider, or coach for children.

The ADHD assessment can include questionnaires, intellectual screenings, rating scales, and sustained attention and distractibility measures. In addition, the medical examiner might want to find out the following about your child:

- How often do they quit a task before eventually completing it?
- How often do they misplace items?
- How often do they forget essential things or instructions?

- Do they have problems with sitting still?
- Do they struggle to relax?
- How often do they get distracted by things around them?

The evaluation for this condition requires a medical history. If a medical exam has not been done recently, the examiner might suggest one ensure the symptoms do not have medical causes. The examiner may also recommend psychological testing to support conclusions and give a more thorough assessment. In some cases, the examiner screen for learning disabilities.

Solution for this disorder, but getting an early diagnosis and treatment is a significant step to improving the lives of the children with this condition and making them have a better experience at school and in life.

4

TALKING TO YOUR CHILD ABOUT ADHD

When your child is diagnosed with ADHD, it is easy to be confused and begin pondering their whole life from that moment. It is also natural for your mind to be worked up with multiple questions about how your child will cope with life's challenges. But every minute you ponder these questions you cannot answer is time wasted, time that would be better put to use in spending quality time with the child, convincing them that their life is not to be derailed by the diagnosis.

Being a parent is enough hard work in the first place, and dealing with this disorder does not make it any easier. But even when faced with this, the responsibility should not be a nightmare. There is enough information and systems to ensure that your child has a good life, but it is up to you to quit worrying and start talking.

At this stage of their life, it is essential to lay down a firm communication structure that allows you to speak to the child about the condition while assuring them of their ability to live a happy, quality life. This is not about lying to them; instead, it is about helping them feel comfortable in their skin, regardless of their condition. Your words and actions have to line up for the conversation.

Understandably, it will be hard to find the right words, and you may struggle with anxiety about discussing this subject with them. However, the child deserves to know why they have struggled emotionally, socially, and academically. They need to understand that it is not their fault they forget things quickly or have no recollection of certain things. You owe it to them to explain why it seems like their life is unmanageable and their affairs are all over the place.

You are the one shot they have at living life as close to normal as possible.

EXPLAINING ADHD TO YOUR CHILD

On average, children are typically diagnosed with ADHD around the seven-year mark. Explaining such a complex topic to a child of that age will be difficult, no doubt, but it is also a crucial step in the right direction for both parent and child.

For starters, you want to speak in a language they will understand. Your vocabulary may be too complex for their reading level, so be sure you are explaining in an age-appropriate way. Avoid the unnecessary details and go in for the age-relevant ones.

You should know that this conversation is not a one-time thing. You must keep updating your child as they mature until they fully grasp the condition. So, please do not rush in with all the details; take your time to deliver it. Not only does this help the child deal with what is happening around them, but it also stokes their curiosity to learn more about themselves.

Here are a few talking points to start with when having the ADHD talk:

- **People with this disorder can also be successful:** Just because they have ADHD does not make them impervious to success. Matter of factly, there are many positive role models making waves with this disorder and carving a niche for themselves. You could start with someone they know, like a family member, friend, or neighbor. Then you could point them to a celebrity, like Jim Carrey, Michael Jordan, Will Smith, Justin Timberlake, Emma Watson, and the list goes on.

- **Having ADHD does not make them flawed:** This disorder should not be seen as a flaw or weakness. It is not a sign that a child is weak or will never amount to anything. The list of celebrities with the condition above demonstrates that success is possible and that these people also lead everyday lives.

The condition makes them a little different from their peers, but it is not a distinguishing flaw. Like any other condition, people with ADHD can have positive experiences and outcomes if given the right support system. Assure them of your presence each step of the way.

- **It is not just them:** ADHD is not a super rare condition that makes your child a unicorn. Not one bit. Over one in every ten children in the United States lives with this disorder. Some sources suggest that the statistics could be 20 percent of the population or one out of every five people.

It can be isolating to think that you are different; hence, alone. But you want to prevent this in your child. Reach out to groups specializing in children with this condition, and help them make friends with other children like them.

An after-school program or summer camp for children with this condition is an excellent place to start. Look for one within your locale so you can still show up for them if they struggle to fit in. In addition, your child will feel less alone in such environments tailored to develop their social and emotional well-being.

- **Having ADHD does not make them dumb:** Granted, they may struggle academically. But this does not mean they are not as bright as their siblings or peers. If the conditions were right, many ADHD children are pretty smart. For example, Thomas Edison and Albert Einstein were two geniuses who contributed to advancing technology and society. Both men had ADHD all their lives but were still regarded as geniuses of their time.

TIPS FOR STARTING THE CONVERSATION

Here are a few tips for a healthy and impactful conversation about ADHD with your child:

- **They may not be interested:** You would expect that, since it is about them, your child would be interested, right? No. They may stare at you blankly or just indulge themselves without paying you any heed. This is especially the case for younger children.

Rather than giving up and leaving them to figure it out on their own, you need to keep trying until they pay attention and are willing to have the conservation.

- **Pick your time well:** Timing is crucial when trying to have a conversation about ADHD. You want to aim for periods when they are less likely to interrupt you. Avoid times when they are interested in other things, like playtime, dinnertime, or bedtime.

Even after finding the right time to impart them, give some time before starting the next conversation. You want them to digest what you spoke about and come up with questions or show understanding in their actions.

- **Avoid dwelling on negatives:** It is easy to get caught up and only focus on the negatives of this condition, but that will not help your child.

Instead, play to their strengths and capabilities. Whether it is their involvement in arts, sports, and science, be willing to give your support and show interest in helping them accomplish more.

- **Open communication is vital:** One conversation is not enough to inform your child about the complexities of ADHD, so do not limit it to one moment. Keep a continuous, open dialogue involving other life areas such as extracurricular activities, friends, school, and homework.
- **Learn more:** If you do not know about ADHD before the diagnosis, you should do your research and learn more about it. Speak to your doctor and get in touch with support and advocacy bodies. Doing so helps you to get in touch with other parents with children like yours, allowing you to learn from them and exchange ideas. It could also be an excellent way to monitor your child's progress through how he interacts with other children.
- **ADHD is not an excuse:** This condition can be made into an excuse for anything, which will only make your child put off things rather than be accountable and deal with them. You want to teach your children that the condition is not a

leeway for destructive behaviors or refusing to put in the work.

TALKING ABOUT THE BRIGHT SIDE

ADHD has various symptoms that interfere with or even disrupt different areas of your child's life. Nonetheless, not all of these symptoms have adverse effects and can be helpful in positive outcomes. This shows that you are getting a mixed bag with the condition.

ADHD has three subtypes, which provoke different symptoms in a child. Some children may only experience impulsive and hyperactive symptoms, others may have inattentive symptoms, and some may have a combination of all three.

Most of the time, we tend to focus on the problems these symptoms cause, and we forget about the unique skills and qualities that trigger in the child. Studies on the subject of this condition show that there are some positives to the condition (Sherrell, 2021). However, these studies were derived from the experiences of people with this condition and not actual scientific studies. Some people involved in the study reported favorable outcomes since their diagnosis.

The Child Neuropsychology journal published a small study in 2006, which identified that sample groups made up of people with this condition were more creative when carrying out specific tasks than other groups without this condition. The task was simple: The researchers asked each participant to draw animals that could be found on another planet that was not Earth. The idea was to create a new toy.

In 2017, another study attempted to examine adults with ADHD and analyze their creativity. The participants were asked to devise new ways of using towels, books, belts, and tin cans.

After the study, both people with and without this condition came up with many ideas. However, the most stunning result was that the people on ADHD medications and those without the disorder showed no differences in creativity.

But it gets interesting.

When the participants were informed that a bonus was at stake for whoever devised the most ideas, people with this condition came out on top. This outcome is not unfounded, as other prior studies also show that competition and rewards hugely influence people with ADHD.

These findings are helpful for several reasons. Most importantly, they enforce the narrative that people with this condition are just as innovative and creative as others without the condition, if not better.

That said, here are some benefits of this condition, as garnered from research over the years:

BENEFITS OF ADHD

- **Increased self-awareness:** People with ADHD often have to monitor their behavior for changes, and most develop a heightened sense of self-awareness. Monitoring their behavior is a crucial part of their day as they manage their disruptiveness.

The negative part of this hyper-self-awareness is that having to do it regularly may reduce their ego and tire them out mentally. However, on the flip side, to prevent this fatigue, they develop a coping mechanism to check and balance themselves effectively.

For people with ADHD, a higher sense of self-awareness helps them understand their needs and feelings while also seeking better ways to properly manage their reactions and behaviors at any given time.

- **Spontaneity:** Impulsivity is one of the critical factors in ADHD. Although it can be a negative behavior that pushes people with the condition to be impatient, cut off others, and act rashly, it is not always a bad thing. People with this condition get progressively better at managing their impulsivity, focusing it instead on new areas and experiences requiring spontaneity.

For these people, finding the balance between boredom and hyperarousal is imperative. So, not only does spontaneity help to spice things up, but it also provides them with enjoyable experiences that take their minds off other distractions.

- **Hyperfocus:** Hyperfocus is another experience for people with this condition. It revolves around channeling all their focus into a subject or task. This behavior can go either way. For one, if they are overly focused on one thing at a time, other areas of their lives may suffer. On the other hand, having hyperfocus ensures that they stay on task, concentrate better, and are more capable of learning better.

Think of this behavior as a "state of flow." Mihály Csíkszentmihályi, a psychologist, defined it as a time of immense focus, absorption, and attention to a task, producing an intense enjoyment.

- **Resilience:** It can be challenging to manage children, more so one with this disorder. So, you must be prepared for the day to face challenges that affect how much they can focus at school or on tasks, manage time and procrastination, take their medication, and manage symptoms that influence their socialization.

Even though it can weigh heavily on you, remember that the challenges are first-hand for your child. But again, that does not make them weak; children with this disorder show remarkable resilience and strength. Resilience has the mental aptitude for dealing with hardship and stress without relying on coping mechanisms, especially negative ones.

A study highlighted that teachers and parents found many children with this disorder to have high resilience in the face of setbacks (Dvorsky, 2016). This makes them more likely to stay on task and achieve their aims, despite difficulties.

- **High energy levels:** Children with this condition are often perceived as rambunctious, especially ones with diagnosed hyperactivity. These high energy levels often manifest as excessive talking, restlessness, and fidgeting.

However, being energetic is not altogether problematic because it can be profitable if used right.

High energy levels are only a problem when unfocused. Otherwise, it is an excellent source of motivation for managing how children with ADHD pursue their goals and stay productive.

Another essential benefit is that children with this condition are better suited for multiple activities (like sports and physical activities) than their peers. They also feel younger, which gives them a positive outlook on life and general well-being.

- **Creativity:** Although children with ADHD may suffer from inattentiveness and distraction, they are not simpletons. As we found from the studies above, they are widely creative, and that is due to their divergent thought processes. Rather than sticking to conventional methods and fixed patterns of problem-solving, they prefer to devise innovative solutions and ideas.

A different study discovered that people with ADHD see themselves as naturally curious, which they consider an upside of the condition (Cherry, 2021). And since curiosity is a crucial part of creativity, curious people are more open and desiring to learn. This way, they can explore newer paths and unique ideas for solving problems.

PUTTING THESE BENEFITS TO GOOD USE

It is not enough to know the benefits. You also want to help your child see these strengths and understand how to use them in the right situations. For example, when they feel very energetic, they can channel their time and effort into a productive venture, like arts and crafts, writing, and exercising. This way, they can flex their minds and bodies while using excess energy. Alternatively, they could try to achieve their goals at school or around the house.

On the other hand, when your child is experiencing hyperfocus, that is the best time to work on a new skill, like learning to code or playing an instrument. Or, you could indulge them in a project, like building a treehouse or redesigning a room around the house; anything to help them channel that focus and find great solutions. It is best to gear them towards activities that promote their creativity, such as talking to a friend, listening to music, or making arts and crafts.

In conclusion, when your child is diagnosed with this condition, it is not the end of their life or normalcy as they know it. Furthermore, the condition does not hamper their chances of success or subsequent growth. On the contrary, if properly managed, ADHD can help your child become one of the best, most successful people on the planet. We have seen this countlessly in the people we celebrate and look up to, from entrepreneurs to media personalities to athletes.

What is more, with advancements in science and the creation of new technologies, ADHD is not as unknown as it used to be. The condition is more manageable now, and there are many resources to improve your understanding of the subject. You can also choose from a range of treatment options for your child. We will get into more details on this in subsequent chapters. This condition is no longer a stumbling block to having a decent and prosperous life.

5

SELF-CARE WHILE DEALING WITH ADHD CHILDREN

As a parent, helping your child overcome challenges is a requirement for the role and an inherent inclination due to your ties with them. This parenting role does not change because a child is diagnosed with ADHD. However, it is crucial now, more than ever, to ensure they have an everyday life. Therefore, many parents are willing to go the extra mile to provide a haven for growth and understanding for their children.

However, while these sacrifices are all well and good, it is easy to forget another person in the picture—*you*. Yes. Even though your child has the condition and not you, it is still imperative that you take good care of yourself. Otherwise, you will not be able to show up for your child as much as they need. And in your zeal, you would have failed them. To take care of your child, you must first be in a great mental and physical position.

To do this, you must set a structure that allows you to catch your breath now and then. Just a moment to reflect and take care of yourself so that you do not let yourself go is critical. You also deserve a happy and fulfilling life, which could double as a great source of motivation for your child.

EFFECTIVE SELF-CARE TIPS FOR PARENTS OF ADHD CHILDREN

When dealing with children with ADHD, life gets cranked up a notch higher. As a result, your well-being can be jeopardized, and you will struggle to maintain both sanity and physical health.

As a result, self-care is key to staying healthy and having your affairs in order before rendering help to your child. This section will go through some effective strategies for safeguarding or restoring your spiritual, physical, and mental health while maintaining healthy living.

Take a Walk

Working out is a great way to keep your mind and body active and fit. However, you will not always have the time to go to the gym or try an intensive workout routine between catering to your child and your other responsibilities. Thankfully, you can still take a walk. A brisk walk or long stroll can help you clear your head and get some air.

It does not matter what you are doing as you walk; you could use the time to get groceries or take your pets for a walk. The goal is to get some energy from being in a neutral setting.

Meditate

A five-minute meditation routine is enough to help calm your body and mind and revitalize your spirits. If you have not tried meditation, you can start with some guided meditation websites or apps. Depending on your device and what you are into, there are several options.

Try breathing exercises to help you manage stress levels as you exercise. This way, you can improve your relaxation without taking too much time by having to nap. Even though taking a few deep breaths does not seem like much, they effectively calm the body and mind.

You can rope your child into some of these activities if you can manage it. For example, meditation can help tone down their high energy levels and improve focus.

Splurge on Yourself

As a parent, it is easy to get caught up with your child and forget that you must be treated right. Do not neglect yourself. The money you make should also go into making you feel good. So, take the time out to splurge a little on yourself.

Get that jacket you have always thought about getting. Change or freshen up your hairdo. Take yourself out to eat. The idea is to do something for yourself, however small. Do not take the liberty to spend more than you should. To ensure you do not exceed any limits, consider adjusting your budget to allow room for saving towards this activity. You deserve to be treated right, so make an effort to do so.

Get Your Laughter On!

Despite how wholesome it can be, laughter is an under-rated part of our society. Your child is going through a lot, and you may be dealing with it regularly, but do not let that rob you of your joy. Laughter helps to improve your immune system and lower stress levels.

So, whip out your phone or laptop and look up some cute and funny videos or memes. Alternatively, watch a comedy show. Just do whatever gets the laugh out of you.

Play Some Music

Music is another part of our culture that plays a role in how we interact with one another or feel. It is a relieving medium of expression for both the singer and listener. In itself, music can be therapeutic.

Create time to listen to music or search for new songs that align with your tastes. Not only is this a great relaxation activity, but it also helps you understand more about yourself.

What's more, music can be enjoyed privately or shared with others. It could be a bonding medium with your child, like when you both have the same favorite song. So kick off your shoes, snuggle into the couch, turn up your music, clear some space, and create a dance floor.

Get a Hug

Hugs are therapeutic and can help to relieve stress and tension. But, of course, not everyone is a hugger. However, we cannot deny that hugs feel good, especially when they are genuine, given, and from people we care about, who also care about us.

So, look around you; walk up to your partner, friend, parent, or child, and give them a good old bear hug. They might not get it at first, but they will hug you all the same.

Practice Mindfulness

To be mindful is to be aware of everything going on around you. Unfortunately, between caring for your child and other life responsibilities, everything outside the fire of your mind can easily blur out. This is not great, as it might relegate other essential things to the background. As a result, practicing mindfulness can help you better delegate your attention to your affairs. Also, it allows you to enjoy the moment better instead of questioning what could have been or the future. This way, you can enjoy what is in front of you and give your child a good life.

Make a Smoothie

Smoothies are great and provide the body with tons of nourishment and fuel, thanks to their protein, greens, and fruit content. Having one can be an excellent way to wind down and get back on track before returning to other activities or caring for your child. It is also a healthier alternative to beverages like coffee or soda.

Get Some Alone Time

For some parents, the only time they are alone is when they use the restroom. This can be a sobering reality, and you do not want that to be your case. Hence, it is recommended that you take some time out to enjoy your own company.

Depending on your spare time, it could be as little as five to ten minutes or as long as several hours. Try not to do anything that does not make you feel relaxed at this point. Now would be a good time to try that smoothie, do some breathing exercises, and practice mindfulness and meditation. The goal is to recharge before delving into work again.

Play Games

Games are great for unwinding, whether mobile games, video games, or board games. Immerse yourself in a game to get your creative juices flowing and enjoy a bit of your competitive edge.

There are many ways to enjoy a game, from playing virtually, by yourself, or playing against family and friends.

Take the Time to Enjoy Nature

Studies identify that spending time in the natural environment improves our psychological health. As little as a hike on a trail, a walk around the park, or just gardening around your yard can make you feel relaxed and rested.

A study was conducted on patients admitted to hospitals with rooms that overlooked green spaces. These patients got better significantly faster than others not placed next to windows with such views. Not only that, but they also reported feeling less anxiety and pain (Ulrich, 1984). This shows that exposure to natural landscapes can offer relief on both mental and physical levels.

Alternatively, you can bring nature into your home with some indoor plants. These plants can be challenging to look after, so be sure about the commitment. Also, if you live along the coast, it could help you visit the beach and splash around.

Savor Something

There is so much to do, and time seems to fly quickly. This rush could likely make you savor things less, so take some time out of your days to savor something. Make it a habit, from little things like having your first cup of Joe for the day to having breakfast with your family. Learn to live in those moments and enjoy them to the fullest.

Keep a Gratitude Journal

Focusing on everything going wrong with you or your child's condition can sometimes make it challenging to be thankful. However, gratitude is not without pay. Studies reveal that people with gratitude journals enjoy better and longer sleep. As a parent, sleep is a precious resource you want to enjoy.

The upside of keeping a gratitude journal is that you do not have to make an entry every day or at defined times; it can be as short as a line of words on any day of the week. In addition, it does not cost a thing and can help you refocus on your prerogatives.

You can make an entry just before bedtime, listing some things you are thankful for. It could be the simplest things or the most sophisticated situations, whatever you want. The general idea is to remind yourself that life is beautiful and there are things to feel good about and be thankful for. This could even be added to your child's bedtime routine to get them to say what they are grateful for.

Make a Retreat in Your Bedroom

Clutter in your bedroom can make you less relaxed and more on edge. So it is understandable if you sometimes feel lazy about putting the clothes away after laundry or cleaning and storing shoes properly.

However, caring for yourself also means preparing your living space to facilitate relaxation. As such, your bedroom is an excellent place to start. Turn it into a retreat that makes you want to come back every time. Throw on those comfy sheets and do a bit of decorating. Place that cozy chair near the window, pry apart the curtains, and settle in with a good book and a glass of wine.

With the room decluttered and aired out, you will find yourself nodding off in no time.

Hold the Electronics

These days, our lives are more digitized than at any other time in history. You could do many things with your gadgets, including surfing the web, browsing social media, or binging shows or streams. While these activities can sometimes be relaxing, they can also lead to more stress and anxiety. This is because digital devices curate pressure, which compels you to do specific tasks, like replying to messages before bedtime or reading those "per the last emails" from work.

While these are not the most arduous tasks, they are mentally tasking. Moreover, they could culminate in a more significant problem over time. So, as a rule of thumb, try a digital detox, in which you steer off of electronics for a bit from time to time. Doing this can help with addiction and be a model for guiding electronic inclinations in your child. Studies show that people who sleep away from their phones get better rest and are generally happier to cement the upsides of the digital detoxification.

Join or Start a Book Club

Book clubs serve myriads of purposes. They can be an excellent medium for meeting other people and starting a social support structure. On the other hand, it could also be the driving force you need to take time to read. Another benefit is that it helps to get you excited for something every other week.

You can start a book club with friends or visit your local library to join one in your locale. There are also online book clubs that you can join, although they are not always great replacements for physical book club meetings. In addition, online book clubs often miss out on traditional book clubs' intimacy and personal touch, making you less motivated to join or keep up.

Create and Achieve a To-Do List

When we talk about caring for ourselves, doing chores does not seem like a relaxing activity. Running errands and cleaning does not seem high up the list of recreational activities, and we understand why. However, checking off items on your to-do list has a lot of relief and is unburdening.

It does not matter what the task is, whether it is decluttering your room, cleaning your bathroom, or booking an appointment for your child. The idea is that making and ticking off your to-do list gives you a sense of accomplishment and something to be thankful for. Moreover, you can go about your to-do list daily, weekly, or monthly. In doing so, you will find a sense of calm in finishing your tasks, rather than procrastinating and leaving them to pile up.

Indulge Your Senses

Life happens whether you are too busy or lazy to bother with it. So, you might as well engage your senses and find inner peace to last you.

Take a long bath, play soothing sounds, light some scented candles, and drink herbal tea. Anything to engage your different senses and bring you to the point of zen, away from the hustle and bustle of day-to-day life, will allow you to relax and decompress.

Spend Time With Family and Friends

Focusing all your time and effort on your ADHD child could rob you of precious moments with other family members and friends. Finding the balance between self-care, caring for your child, and hanging out with family and friends can be challenging. But you owe it to yourself and them to try.

Including me time in your schedule is essential. This way, you can plan toward it without compromising other essential things. This is a great self-care tip for balancing your affiliations and avoiding the stress of strained relationships.

PARENTING TIPS FOR SINGLE PARENTS ON RAISING ADHD CHILDREN

- **Do your homework:** ADHD can be a genetic matter sometimes. If your child has the condition, there is a 30 to 40 percent chance that either you or your partner has ADHD. If left untreated, the condition can make effective parenting difficult, if not impossible, especially in the case of single-parent households. The symptoms of untreated ADHD make it hard for the child to be organized, keep to a schedule, and maintain consistency. If you are concerned about your ADHD status, consider talking to your primary health care provider for diagnosis and advice.
- **Schedule family meetings regularly:** Plan for weekly family meetings with your children. The assembly aims to discuss a specific topic. Encourage your family members to make conscious decisions to contribute to the creation of the agenda, and put rules in place to ensure everyone gets some time to air their views. You want the meeting to be solution-

centric and productive, and it is best when everyone is a part of the process.
- **Highlight everyday stressors:** We all have unique stressors that impact our quality of life. You must avoid or limit your stressor to make the most of your time. For instance, a stressor may involve taking on other people's tasks because you cannot say "no." While you cannot control how they will respond to being denied, you must also look out for yourself to avoid burnout and overwhelm.

Granted, there will be stressors that you cannot just nope out of. However, in such cases, it helps to refocus on the positives and identify helpful coping mechanisms to deal with the stress. For example, start with some deep breaths, and delay your response to avoid impulsive reactions. You can also try meditative and relaxing routines or exercises that reduce stress levels.

- **Talk about chores:** As a single parent, it is easy to be caught up in household chores every other day without delegating. But it does not have to be so. Involving your children in chores can be a positive experience for bonding and skill acquisition. Not only do they get practical life skills, but they also develop good work ethics and a sense of responsibility.

On the other hand, delegating chores will open up more time for you to focus on other things. Also, over time, your child will get used to the routine and not require oversight anymore.

- **Get the proper support:** It takes a lot of effort to raise a child, so you may want to get a solid support structure around you. Identify key family members, support groups, friends, and babysitters who will help you nurture your child properly.
- **Create some one-on-one time:** Finding the time to squeeze another appointment or task into your already crammed schedule may threaten to send everything flying. However, it cannot be helped that your child requires some one-on-one time with you to reconnect and develop your relationship. This time spent together is especially crucial for children with ADHD, who could sometimes experience negative spells in which they feel unwanted or low on confidence. You could build up their self-esteem with one-on-one time and teach them to feel better about themselves.

- **Create to-do lists:** Every day is an excellent day to make and follow a to-do list. However, in making plans for the day, learn to be reasonable in your expectations. Do not expect to summit Everest and make it in time for dinner on the same day. Leave enough room for unforeseen contingencies.
- **Create routines and set clear rules:** Create house routines and follow them religiously. Not only will this make your days more predictable and easy to follow, but it will also help your child follow instructions better. This benefit is especially helpful for children with ADHD, as they perform better in situations with consistent and straightforward rules.

When devising rules and routines for your household, it is best to partner with your child. First, discuss possible repercussions for certain behaviors if your child's other parent is still in the picture. Then, partner with them to create a consistent environment geared towards the convenience of both parties and the child. This way, everyone knows visiting times and can plan their schedules around it, making room for contingency.

Otherwise, if the other parent is not involved, you may want to bring your child's doctor into the picture. Plan around hospital visits, checkups, and other health plans.

HANDLING MARITAL LIFE

Raising a child with ADHD can make you feel disconnected from many things, including your marriage, which can strain your relationship with your significant other. Hence, it is crucial to take some time out to focus on your marriage. Remember that raising a child is the job of both parents, so you do not want to commit too much and go in alone. This will save you unnecessary marital problems.

Also, as much as your friends will understand not reaching out consistently, you should try to reciprocate the gesture by sending out a message often. It does not have to be anything special or nifty; just checking up on them and listening to the goings-on in their lives can keep the friendship going for longer. Your child's condition is not enough reason to abandon all forms of normalcy in your life. If your child is to believe that their life is still on track, you cannot afford to let yours get derailed.

That said, here are some practical tips to help you maintain your marriage when dealing with children with ADHD:

- **Take turns:** As a couple, taking care of your ADHD child can be easier if you go in turns. This way, everyone gets a break at some point from the child and one another. Understanding how this sounds, you could mistake it for troubling signs, but it is not. Too much of everything is bad, even the company of someone you truly care about. You are taking the time to refresh both mind and body, providing you with much-needed balance, which can be hard to come by in a family setting.
- **Do not fly solo:** Just as you both have to take turns with your child, you also have to split parenting responsibilities. Doing so makes things easier on both parents and reduces the risk of resentments and conflicts, which could sour relationships.
- **Adaptability is key:** Your child's ADHD status will not change in a heartbeat, so it would help you learn to cope. Find ways around the suitable condition for the child, your partner, and you.
- **Streamlined intents:** It is challenging to raise a child with ADHD, and you do not want to add marital problems to the list. Working together instead of trying to one-up each other provides

the best chance of helping the child have a better life. So, try to avoid blaming each other for shortcomings. In the end, you are both ordinary people just trying to do right by your child, however tasking it seems. The odds of success are way better when there is coordination and unity of efforts.

- **Set clear house rules:** Plan and agree on house rules with your significant other. Being on the same page creates a better avenue for raising your children, including ones with and without ADHD. Clear-cut rules also help to prevent a clash of interests, as everyone knows, understands, and accepts the rules of engagement.
- **Go on a vacation or take an extended break:** Fit in some couple time into your schedule. You and your significant other must grow your relationship away from the children.

In conclusion, raising children with ADHD is tasking and affects your physical and mental health. From their impulsiveness to their reluctance to obey, it can make it frustrating to perform your responsibilities, and you may sometimes be seething in anger. Other times, you may feel guilty for going hard on them, especially as the condition has a hand in their behavior. It is for this reason that you ought to practice self-care. The pressure gets intense sometimes, and you need an outlet to de-stress and refocus your priorities. However, to be there for your child, you first have to be responsible for yourself.

Furthermore, in your quest for self-care, do not forget to practice your virtues. For example, love and compassion are crucial when dealing with children with ADHD. Because when all else fails, these virtues will help you through.

A Welcome Break

"Be kind to others, so that you may learn the secret art of being kind to yourself." - Paramahansa Yogananda

Let's take a break.

It feels good, doesn't it? Just a moment to take a breath without taking in any new information or having to handle a situation with the kids.

You probably don't get many of these moments. Not many parents of children with ADHD do. So it's important that you do give yourself a break - both in terms of how much you expect of yourself, and in the practical sense. Those self-care tips in Chapter 5 are important. don't be tempted to skip them because they don't seem to directly relate to your child.

Take a moment, too, to acknowledge the extra work you're putting in to help your child and your own journey as a parent. You don't have a lot of time, but you're here now, with this book. Don't be hard on yourself if you can't read the whole thing. Your life is full, and you're doing everything you can.

Nonetheless, if you'd like to make this break last a moment longer, you have a glorious opportunity to help out other parents of children with ADHD.

By leaving a review of this book on Amazon, you'll help other parents who are looking for this guidance to find it quickly and easily.

No matter how much you've read, sharing how it has helped you and what information you've found here will signpost to other new readers with limited time and energy where they can find the help they're looking for.

You're doing an amazing job. Thank you for helping me to make sure other parents know they are too.

6

PARENTING STRATEGIES FOR HELPING YOUR ADHD CHILD - AT HOME

At this point, it is pretty clear that raising children with ADHD is a different ballgame from raising children without the condition. The challenges are more severe and require carefully crafted strategies for navigating the child's day-to-day life and how they turn out. However, even at that, knowing what to do is the easiest part.

For starters, you must understand that there are biological differences between the brains of a child with and without ADHD. Of course, your ADHD child can comprehend discipline and learn to organize themselves and their affairs, but that does not make them any less susceptible to impulsive behaviors. On the contrary, the condition makes them likely to do things on a whim or without care or focus. Furthermore, if you think that will not bother you, you lie.

As discussed in the previous chapter, self-care comes first in raising a child with ADHD. It helps you be there for them at all times. However, that is not the end of it. You also need to know the dos and don'ts of parenting ADHD children so that you do not complicate things for them or yourself.

PRO-PARENTING TIPS FOR RAISING ADHD CHILDREN

As the parent of a child with ADHD, one word you repeatedly hear is structure. But why? What has structure got to do with a cognitive condition? Simple: Structure provides a predictable and organized environment—two critical factors in raising a child with ADHD. Creating an organized environment involves planning a schedule and daily routines for your child. However, on the other hand, a predictable environment has expectations, rules, and repercussions that are known and understood by the child through positive reinforcement.

Think of a structured environment like scaffolding. Every limit, reminder, and routine you set up contributes to the upward growth of the building, which, in this case, is the child with ADHD. Scaffolding may not be the prettiest sight, but its importance to the solidity of the structure cannot be understated.

A structured environment is ideal for children with ADHD because they know what to expect at any one time. It is this understanding that provides them with a sense of security. The result of such an environment is evident in children with and without ADHD because they grow up with better self-awareness and knowledge of how the world works.

However, this does not mean that children are incapable of self-structuring; far from it. Many children devise their structure for tasks, chores, and schedules and exhibit good behaviors without being prompted. Things are different for children with ADHD, though. Self-structuring is more challenging due to the disorders of the condition. They struggle to regulate their emotions and responses and have poor organizational skills. For them, maintaining focus and avoiding impulsive behaviors is a chore, especially with the many distractions begging for their attention.

ADHD symptoms are primarily connected to their problems with self-control. Therefore, children with ADHD require better external structures or control systems to manage their symptoms, stay grounded at all times, and serve as a stepping stone for other helpful strategies.

That said, here are some tips for creating an effective and lasting structure:

- **Manage their sleep cycle:** Children with ADHD have a problematic bedtime routine, no thanks to their condition. The inability to fall asleep quickly worsens other symptoms of the condition, like recklessness, hyperactivity, and inattention. As such, it is vital to help your child navigate sleep. You must remove potential inhibitors, such as caffeine, sugar, and screen time to do that. Create a bedtime ritual that calms their senses and helps them relax.
- **Decide on acceptable and unacceptable behaviors:** A structured environment aims to help your child understand the consequences of their actions and manage their inclinations to act impulsively. Creating one requires strength, affection, empathy, energy, and patience. Start by deciding on behaviors that may or may not be tolerated. Ensure the child is aware of these behaviors, and do your best to enforce them.

Punishing ADHD children is complicated as many do not mind having things taken away from them. When your child breaks the rules, talk to them first and ask questions such as, what rule is it that you broke? Why did you break this rule? What can you do next time to avoid breaking this rule? This is not to say that you should care for your child with an iron fist. Instead, it is to ensure consistency and safeguard the child's improvement.

Certain behaviors should not be excused, like refusing to turn off the TV, staying off screens before bedtime, or being reluctant to get up in the morning. Of course, it would take some getting used to for the child to internalize all the rules, but they will over time. To further aid this process, make the rules as clear and straightforward as can be, with rewards to foster good behavior.

- **Have faith in your child:** Create a list of everything you find unique, positive, and valuable in your child. Have faith in them that regardless of their condition, they are capable of changing, succeeding, learning, and maturing. Moreover, as you wake up and prepare them for the future daily, reaffirm this belief and help them believe it, too.
- **Tone down distractions:** Children with ADHD are often subject to distractions around them, such as video games, computers, or television.

These gadgets encourage them to be impulsive and must be regulated. Start with some decreased screen time while subsequently increasing their time on other engaging activities with family and friends or outside of the home. The goal is to help them use pent-up energy.

- **Deal with aggression:** Children with ADHD often experience aggressive outbursts, which can be challenging for parents. Instead of clapping back at them, consider other healthier alternatives, like a time-out to help calm both parties. Acting out is not limited to home life alone and could sometimes happen in public. In such a case, removing them calmly and quickly is imperative. Explain what time-out means, and teach them to ruminate on their actions.

Only consider time-outs for negative behaviors, as mild disruptions may be a means of releasing built-up energy. Also, when they behave destructively, intentionally, or abusively, it goes against the rules and demands to be addressed.

- **Encourage them to voice their thoughts:** Self-control is a problem for many children with ADHD and makes them prone to impulsive actions and utterances long before considering the aftereffects. As a result, asking your child to voice their thoughts when they feel the urge to act disruptively could help. Doing so will better comprehend their thought processes and help them work out positive coping mechanisms.

- **Make your child's life organized and simple:** Design a little quiet area where they can indulge themselves, do homework, or take a break when things become overwhelming for them. Think of it as their special place. Also, keep the house clean and organized, so the child knows the location of whatever they need. Doing so can also help lessen physical distractions around the house.

- **Make the rules clear, but do not be too rigid:** One way to help your child adapt to rules is by regularly discouraging negative behaviors and rewarding good ones. In doing so, do not forget that children with ADHD do not have the same adaptability as other children. So, be flexible enough to allow room for mistakes and learning on the go.

If they exhibit odd behaviors that do not impact them negatively, accept them as some of the influences of their condition. However, on the other hand, discouraging quirky behaviors you do not understand because they do not seem "normal" to you is pretty harmful.

- **Encourage physical activities:** Engaging in physical activities is suitable for using excess energy. It also allows the child to channel their focus into well-defined movements that could bring about low impulsive reactions. Exercising also boosts concentration, improves brain function and memory, and lowers the risk of anxiety and depression. There are many professional athletes with ADHD, but the condition does not get in their way. Experts suggest that children with ADHD learn to focus their energy, attention, and passion by exercising.
- **Get personalized counseling:** It is impossible to be everything your child with ADHD needs. Sure, you can provide for and nurture them, but you cannot also offer the professional help they require from time to time. It is time to get a therapist for your child who will give them a new outlet to let off steam. It can be challenging dealing with the fact that you cannot come through in every way for your child, but seeking assistance is not a weakness.

A therapist will also come in handy for lowering your anxiety and stress levels by providing you with professional insights. You can also join local support groups for parents of ADHD children.

- **Split tasks into smaller bits:** Map out a plan for the activities delegated to your child. Use a large calendar and color coding to highlight chores and when they are due. Doing so gives your child the predictability of knowing what to do next. It also helps bridge their focus and channel it into their day-to-day routines.

WHAT PARENTS SHOULD NOT DO

- **Please do not give in to the child or the condition:** As a parent, allowing your child to get away with everything because they have ADHD can start a slippery slope. You need to set rules for acceptable behavior and enforce them. This is not to say that all nurture, care, and patience go out the window. Not at all. Instead, it is simply that you should not set the bar so low that your child becomes a nuisance.
- **Avoid overwhelm:** Keep in mind that ADHD influences how your child behaves. So, even though the condition is not visible, it is still a

disability that affects them and their choices. When things get heated, it is time to take a deep breath and remember that your child is not deliberately trying to push all your buttons.

- **Relax on the little details:** Do not be too rigid with your child. Allow room for some flexibility or "bending" of the rules. For instance, if they had done three of the five chores, do not come down hard on them to finish the remaining two in record time. Remember, they are learning to live within a structured environment, and every step in the right direction is progress. Remember to praise them for what they did accomplish. You can certainly talk to them about the remaining two chores and ask for a plan for when they will be done. Everyone needs skills in life, so treating your child with respect and having an open line of communication is a great building block for them.

- **Avoid negativity:** As simple as it sounds; you may sometimes feel tempted to rush through things. Avoid such inclinations. Take things one at a time to avoid losing sight of what matters: Your child's healthy development. Anything embarrassing or stressful that they did today will not matter tomorrow.

TEACHING HYGIENE TO YOUR ADHD CHILD

Just because a task does not seem like a big deal for you does not mean your child is living the same experience, especially when they have ADHD. Getting children with the condition to do basic hygienic tasks like helping with the dishes, taking out the trash, or tidying up their rooms can be challenging. You may be torn between deciding to let them off easy without chores or wondering why they do not bother to help at all. Neither option is good. Understand that your child is looking for guidance, and it may be that they just need your help to stay focused. So while you may not be doing the chore, you are there to guide or help keep them on track. For example, leaving a child to clean their room will likely make it messier. What if you were in the room, hanging out on the bed, talking to them, and guiding them on how to clean their room appropriately? Or understand that asking for an entire room to be cleaned in one set without breaks or even broken up in multiple days is not the best of ideas. Remember, ADHD children do not have a long attention span for things that do not interest them.

Not letting them participate in chores disrupts the structure you are trying to build around them. On the other hand, their refusal to help is not necessarily born out of disregard, so remember that. You need to adjust how you approach the subject of chores. For starters, always be direct and specific with whatever tasks you want them to do, and state any incentives that might bolster their cooperation.

Another thing you want to incorporate is listing. Lists help children with ADHD track their activities and give them the predictability of knowing what to do next. So, instead of just stating what you want them to do, make a to-do list and paste it on a wall. Now, they do not have to deal with trying to remember the chores. Furthermore, you can break down each task into smaller components. For example, instead of just writing, "tidy your room," try "fold the laundry into the drawers," "bring dirty clothes to the laundry room," or "make your bed." The details here make it much easier to work with.

A chore chart is another technique that can help familiarize your ADHD child with household activities. Unlike the to-do list, a chore chart involves chores, a breakdown of each one, the time of completion, and what they can expect to get. Think of it as a mini treasure map with tasks to access the gold. For smaller children, stickers or points further drive home the idea of chores and makes them even more interested. A behavioral contract may be more beneficial for older children (including teenagers) than a chore chart. The difference is that they are involved in the creation process. Call a meeting to review acceptable and unacceptable behaviors and rewards and punishments. Agree, and sign it.

Stickers, points, and rewards are all incentives to guide your child down the right path. For example, with a point system, the child accumulates them from performing assigned chores. In turn, they are rewarded with outings, privileges, or activities agreed upon prior. Also, decide on how much they can use these points. For children under seven, two to three times a week is excellent.

For children between seven and ten, once a week works fine. The goal of the reward system is to provide a positive incentive for the child's behavior. It is better to reward well-done jobs than punish incomplete ones. For every task completed, tick the chart or place a star on it to remind your child of what they stand to gain for good behavior.

Lastly, do not hover around eager to help when setting up tasks for your children. Sometimes, let them figure things out on their own. Of course, be within reaching distance for when they need your help and ensure they do not get distracted and steered away from the task at hand. However, do not interfere too much and make them dependent on your presence. One way to help them grow independent is to take a picture before and after doing a task, like cleaning up their room. It could also help them become more confident in their abilities.

In conclusion, making plans for regulating how your child behaves is an essential step in creating a support system that facilitates growth and organization. It will not be easy because children with ADHD often prove challenging to manage. However, you should be okay with the proper behavioral techniques and structure.

7

PARENTING STRATEGIES FOR HELPING YOUR ADHD CHILD - AT SCHOOL

ADHD plagues focus and attention, making children more susceptible to impulsive and destructive behaviors. In turn, these behaviors lead them into trouble, which is why many children with ADHD struggle to have good relationships with their peers. Unfortunately, their conditions also make them prime targets for classroom nuisance, even when they are relatively quiet and innocent.

But all is not lost. Here are some strategies for aiding your child to improve at school and rise to the occasion when called upon.

EXECUTIVE FUNCTION

An executive function is a series of cognitive skills needed for discipline and self-control. It is also a cognitive process responsible for managing tasks and thoughts, decision-making, prioritizing activities, and effective time management. Executive function skills aid in establishing strategies and skills for handling projects. It also determines how we act to move forward with each task. People without executive function struggle with organizing, analyzing, scheduling, planning, completing tasks—or working with deadlines. They quickly lose track of time, misplace things, suffer overwhelm from tasking projects, and prioritize the wrong things.

There is confusion surrounding this subject and how it concerns people with ADHD. For example, an ADHD be classified as an executive function disorder? Or are all executive function disorders ADHD? The answers to these questions depend on how we define executive functions and their role in self-regulation.

Karl Pribram first used executive functioning in the 1970s. His studies suggested that the prefrontal cortex is primarily responsible for mediating executive functions. Traditional medicine has seen the subject applied immensely in clinical psychology, psychiatry, and neuropsychology. However, executive functioning has evolved into a broader topic discussed in education and general psychology. It has been integrated into classroom accommodations and teaching strategies.

There are seven core self-regulation types affiliated with executive functioning. They include:

- **Self-motivation:** Pushing yourself to accomplish things without extrinsic motivation or consequences
- **Nonverbal working memory:** Making mental notes for behavioral guidance
- **Emotional:** Integrating images, words, and self-awareness to influence your feelings on certain subjects
- **Problem-solving and planning:** Identifying new and innovative solutions and paths
- **Self-restraint:** Constraining yourself
- **Verbal working memory:** Maintaining internal dialogue
- **Self-awareness:** Turning the spotlight on yourself

The Four Circuits of Executive Function

Looking at ADHD from these circuits' perspectives helps us understand the origin of specific symptoms. Variations in symptoms affecting a child with ADHD depend on the level of impairment seen in these circuits. For example, some children have higher emotional regulation issues while others have higher working memory deficits. Some may experience challenges with time management but are much better at other things. Whatever the case, each of these circuits explained below comes into play:

- **The Who Circuit:** This circuit covers the area stretching from the frontal lobe to the back of the hemisphere. It is responsible for self-awareness and regulates the goings-on around us, how we feel, and what we do, both internally and externally.
- **The When Circuit:** The when circuit connects from the prefrontal areas of the brain to one of the oldest areas, known as the cerebellum, which is one of the backmost parts of the brain. This circuit is responsible for timing and regulates the sequence of behaviors and how seamlessly they are performed. It also coordinates the timeliness of actions and the decisive time of doing anything. A dysfunction

in the when circuit, especially in people with ADHD, is responsible for their inability to manage time judiciously.

- **The What Circuit:** This circuit runs from the frontal lobe's outer surface to the brain's area known as the basal ganglia—or, more precisely, the striatum. This circuit is responsible for working and adequate memory, so it manages the thoughts that guide our actions. This is especially the case for making plans, setting goals, and cogitating about the future.

- **The Why Circuit:** This circuit also begins from the frontal lobe and passes through the central area of the brain called the anterior cingulate. It ends in the amygdala, the limbic system's primary gateway. The circuit is considered the "hot" circuit because it is directly in charge of emotions. It regulates how our thoughts influence our feelings and vice versa. It is also primarily responsible for decision-making, particularly in planning. When deciding between several options, the why circuit comes into play to help single out an option among all others based on their motivational and emotional properties and how they make us feel.

The Development of Executive Functions

Abilities linked to executive functioning develop at different paces from one another. The development process is sequential, with one skill developing off the back of another. Every type of executive function interacts with one another. It plays a role in the regulation of behaviors in individuals to lead to desired outcomes in the future.

The development of executive functions begins at age two and continues until age 30 when they become fully developed. However, people with ADHD often experience delayed development by 30 to 49 percent, making them more inclined to be driven by short-term goals instead of long-term ones.

The back regions of the brain are in charge of information storage about everything one learns. On the other hand, the front area is where the stored information is used for social effect and success in life. This shows how the prefrontal cortex mediates executive functions through the four primary circuits.

People experiencing executive functioning challenges—especially those with ADHD—may suffer impairments in one or more of the discussed circuits. As a result, such people may experience dysfunction in terms of social skills, planning, touch memory, and emotional regulation.

To better understand the executive dysfunctions in your child, do your homework on the subject and find out the best interventions and therapies that could help. Also, get in touch with your child's doctor once you begin noticing symptoms, including, but not limited to, the ones discussed below.

Symptoms of Executive Dysfunction

People with executive functioning difficulties may be subject to any or several of these symptoms:

- The trouble with creating schedules and organizing things
- Poor time management, or the inability to make plans while also taking cognizance of future activities
- Problems with processing and analyzing information
- Challenges with coordinating actions to achieve long-term goals
- The trouble with managing impulses and emotions

On the other hand, when there are no defects in executive functioning, people tend to:

- Complete activities in a timely fashion
- Coordinate the steps necessary for performing tasks
- Effectively analyze and process tasks
- Make adjustments or shifts as needed to complete activities
- Make plans for addressing goals
- Create timelines for achieving goals

How Executive Function Impacts Children With ADHD

The connection between ADHD and executive functions is that the latter develops as a result of impairments in the former, which is the self-management module of the brain. So, while people without ADHD can suffer from impairments in executive function, people with the condition suffer from several executive function impairments.

These six clusters of executive functions are often impaired in attention deficit hyperactivity disorder:

- **Action:** Tracking and managing physical activities

- **Emotion:** Dealing with frustrating and regulating feelings
- **Activation:** Organizing activities and materials, time management, and starting tasks
- **Effort:** Analyzing speed, maintaining driving force, and managing alertness
- **Memory:** Accessing recall and using working memory
- **Focus:** Identifying, maintaining, and alternating attention when necessary

Executive dysfunctions are sometimes hereditary, especially in children with ADHD. Nevertheless, there is also a chance that damage could cause in the prefrontal cortex, severe neglect, in vitro exposure to harmful substances, and trauma. One study discovered that people susceptible to impairments in executive functioning typically suffer from injuries, disorders, damage, or disease to the same area as the brain.

Managing Problems With Executive Function

Executive function problems can also stem from learning disabilities and disorders in executive function. Whatever the case, the reason for managing issues with the condition is to help strengthen executive function skills, which are otherwise deficient in the affected individual. Put simply: The primary goal is to work out the problem.

The management process is individualized and dependent on the areas that require more attention and the underlying reason for the dysfunction. However, according to the National Center for Learning Disabilities (NLCD), here are some general tips to help improve problems with executive function:

- Create routines and plan shifts and transition periods for activities
- Set up visual task aids or visual schedules, like a flow chart of activity milestones, and go over them multiple times daily
- Use a step-by-step approach to work by splitting tasks into more minor activities.
- Ask for written guides or oral guidance as much as possible.
- Use tools like alarm watches, computers, or organizers to track time and stay on course

Using these strategies can help you manage the issue in your child before, during, and after seeking medical counsel. Not only will it make their life much easier, but they will also not be easily overwhelmed with little tasks.

PARENTING TIPS FOR HELPING YOUR ADHD CHILD AT SCHOOL

- **Please do your homework:** It is crucial to know the policies, regulations, and laws safeguarding the health of your child, as well as the rights the child has. Two federal laws ensure that children with disabilities receive "free and appropriate education." The first is Section 504 of the Rehabilitation Act of 1973, and the second is the Individuals with Disabilities Education Act (IDEA).

Both rules require schools to provide the necessary infrastructure and services to aid learning. There may even be other laws unique to your state. Find out about them; you want the law on your side.

- **Learn about the Individualized Education Program (IEP):** If your child with ADHD needs something different from what is taught in school, or a new way to learn things, it is best to give them an IEP. Not only does an IEP satisfy these needs, but it also shows you how to track their progress offering insights on the type of service to expect from the school. The school is expected to meet with parents twice a year to review the IEP. The first review is establishing the IEP and what needs to be included. The second meeting is to review the goals and how your child performs. You must stay very involved with the IEP and ensure that all teachers adhere. An IEP can follow your child through college and update throughout the school years, but it is imperative to remain involved, so your child has their needs met.

- **Find out the policies and support that apply to your child at their school:** Send a written note to the principal of your child's school requesting an evaluation of their services and policies. If you want to learn more about how to go about this letter, consider visiting the Children and Adults with Attention Deficit Hyperactivity Disorder (CHADD) website for samples.

Some schools, especially public ones, offer social skill groups—small gatherings of two to eight children led by a speech therapist or the school's psychologist. The group teaches children to manage specific social situations and connect with their peers.

- Know the 504 plan: If an IEP is unnecessary for your child—who will remain in the same class as other students on the same grade level—you might need a 504 plan. This document shows how the school supports your child, with each plan designed to meet the child's needs. While class lessons will remain relatively unchanged in this case, you can expect the following privileges for your child:

- Counseling, occupational therapy, or speech therapy
- Providing verbal answers in a test as opposed to writing them down
- Getting more time to complete schoolwork and tests
- Attempting tests in a different room than others or with fewer students to limit the chance of distractions
- Having the option to skip reading and use audiobooks instead

However, there are no rigid laws on obtaining a 504 plan, so it is up to your child's school. If you feel the plan would be helpful for your child, reach out to your local school district and learn the terms involved.

- **Speak to teachers:** Regularly meet up with your child's teacher to discuss their goals and needs and how best they can be helped in class.

This could mean relocating your child's seat from the windows and doors to the front of the course. This way, they can remain focused and avoid distractions. The teacher can also come in to offer a little help. Request access to the school schedule, so you do not catch the teacher at the wrong time.

This is also handy for tracking your child's progress. If you can help it, getting another set of books for your child to use at home can help. In doing so, you can learn how best they learn and relay it to the teacher.

- **Work together:** It would help to work with your child's teacher instead of trying to impose on them. Your child will take it as a sign that the adults in their life want the best for them.
- **Be coordinated:** Parent-teacher meetings are often kept short so parents can ask questions. When attending, come prepared to ask vital questions. Organize all the necessary details, including test results, teacher notes, and report cards, in a binder for easy reference.
- **Do not get offensive:** Occasionally, you may be called about your child not paying attention in class or disrupting class activities. It is easy to give the caller a piece of your mind at that

moment. Instead, reach out to them about your child's condition. Explain that you know how much of a handful your child can be, and suggest possible solutions. Simply providing the child with directions for a task or changing their seating setup can help.

- **Speak regularly:** Keep in touch with your child's teacher by mail, phone calls, and in person. By doing this, you can find out how your child is progressing, how they deal with schoolwork, and if they are adjusting to changes. You could also learn about the assignments your child brings home and ask for help. This way, you can ensure that your child can go through the homework independently or request extra time on tests.

Visit the teacher's website to learn about projects, upcoming tests, and exams. Seek the teacher's advice on how to help your child prepare for the due dates and organize their stuff outside the classroom. This can save you from dealing with meltdowns at the last moment.

- **Approach cautiously:** Be careful how you approach teachers to avoid putting them on the defensive. For instance, rather than asking,

"Why don't you help John Doe when he struggles with classwork?" say, "I fear that John Doe may be struggling to finish classwork. How can we help him stay focused so he does not fall behind on his studies?"

- **Create mutual goals:** Your child manifests and is influenced by ADHD symptoms in and outside school. So, say they struggle to follow directions; try discussing with the teacher some new means of keeping the child grounded and onboard. The solution must be practical both at home and in school.
- **Express gratitude:** When teachers go out of their way to understand your child and aid them in learning, be appreciative. Send a note to express your appreciation or visit in person.
- **Discuss in person:** Plan your schedule to include meeting times with your child's teacher. Each meeting should be set up around the early stages of the school year. Stick to the plan and meet up to discuss your child's situation. During the meeting, remain courteous and cheerful. Do not focus on the problems alone.

Instead, talk about creating solutions. For example, do not say, "Jane Doe, she is headstrong." Instead, say, "I have noticed that Jane Doe does not like to ask for help if others are around but will ask if she can talk quietly with someone." Any other educational plans or reports should also be shared in the meeting.

- **Join the conversation:** Volunteer at the school, chaperone an event, attend back-to-school events and offer to help with the library. Little pitching-ins show the school and the teacher that you are committed to your child's growth. You will also get insights into how your child interacts outside the home.
- **Please keep your child's teachers informed:** Since you are bringing them into the process, there is no need to cherry-pick the details that teachers should know. Inform them if your child starts or changes ADHD medications. This way, they can look out for side effects and provide you with feedback on whether or not the meds are helping the child. You also want to keep them in the loop on significant household changes that could affect your children, such as the birth of a baby, a death in the family, or divorce.
- **Getting started at a new school:** As mentioned above, children with ADHD are often hardest hit by significant changes. So, whether relocating during the summer or beginning the

first year of middle or high school, you want to ease the burden on them. For a start, reach out to the school beforehand. This way, the new school can pair your child with teachers and classes suited to every learning style and ability.

- **Learn more:** Call the school early on and plan to send your child's report cards, notes, and test scores from the previous school. Schedule a meeting with your child's teacher and the guidance counselor. At the same time, go over the IEP or 504 plan to see if you need a new one.
- **Petition the guidance counselor to give you and your child a tour of the school:** Get to know the school nurse, the teachers, the principal, and other vital people your child will meet. Help your child get used to the roads by walking them around the premises. If you can manage it, arrange a hangout or playdate with another student from their new class.
- **Create plans and routines:** Create plans, routines, and practices to help your child adjust to the changes and feel better on their first day.

HELPING YOUR CHILD WITH THEIR HOMEWORK

Not many children are huge fans of homework. And rightly so, too. For children with ADHD, homework routines seem monumental. It is enough hard work writing down the assignment and bringing home the necessary information to accomplish the task. As a result, they tend to lose some papers either on their way home, at home, or on the way to school.

Sometimes, it is a different ball game, and they do not even bother attempting the assignment. For example, suppose the homework makes it home in one piece. In that case, they find the effort needed to focus on the work, recall the instructions, and understand the assignment hard to come by. Moreover, with all the distractions floating around, there is much to focus on. As a result, much homework does not get turned in, and the ones that attract poor grades. This can lower the self-esteem of the child, making them feel incompetent. They also start to despair and are easily hurt by criticisms for their behaviors.

As a parent, we want to help them do better. So here are some simple but practical tips for getting around this hurdle:

- **Color coding:** Color coding is a great way to help organize and can go a long way with ADHD children. So, the next time you are getting them an assignment notebook, get different colored book covers, pens, notebooks, and folders. Designate each color to a specific subject. Finally, get another lockable folder for storing homework papers. This way, your child will have a permanent location for accessing homework files. It will also improve their organizational skills and make them less likely to lose assignments.
- **Offer support and tools:** Take your child shopping to pick a notebook of their choice for writing down homework assignments from school. Get in touch with their teachers to issue verbal reminders about the assignments and give them time to take notes. Furthermore, you could inquire about how homework is issued. You can solicit the teacher to begin doing so if it is not written on the board. Such a change will benefit both your child and the entire class.

You can also prime the teachers to look out for your child and ensure they maintain focus and take down assignments as instructed. Moreover, when they are distracted, a quick tap on the shoulder should be enough to redirect their attention without embarrassing them. Teachers could also go through the assignment notebook by the end of class to ensure the accuracy of the writing. Finally, you could ask for a weekly schedule of the assignments at home as a backup.

- **Acknowledge efforts:** As your child goes through their assignments, endeavor to be relaxed and positive all the way through. The time is right to offer feedback on their hard work and efforts. During mealtimes, compliment them before other family members. It is easy to get caught up with the negatives of ADHD and forget that your child is also human and in need of acknowledgment. Do not hesitate to point out when they are doing well. If they behave well until the end of the week, you could even take them out to someplace special to celebrate.
- **Arrange their backpacks:** Join your child in arranging their backpack. As they offload their books for assignments, teach them how to clean their bags. Start with old, unnecessary items they hoard in some areas. This way, you will not have to deal with moldy leftovers or snacks they forgot to eat several weeks back. Doing so

also helps to organize the items in the bag, which makes for fewer distractions for the child. While this activity may appear trivial, offering your child with ADHD extra guidance and support goes a long way for them.

- **Be your child's advocate:** Do not be afraid to set up meetings with your child's teachers to talk about any concerns you may have about their homework. Granted, it will not always be possible to see all teachers attend to your child. For such cases, use other means, like phone calls or emails.

If possible, teachers may be willing to reduce the assignment workload your child has to deal with. Of course, the change will be subtle, so their peers do not see it. For instance, if a mathematics assignment requires the class to attempt 30 questions, your child may only have to do 15. To set this up, get in touch with their teachers and speak about giving the child extended time or reduced workloads.

- **Medication:** If your child is on meds, remember that the drug may have worn off towards late afternoon, which is usually the time for homework. Consult your child's doctor to find out if you can withhold one of the medication dosages until homework time. Ensure your child does not get the medicine too late, as it could affect their sleep.

- **Maintain a pseudo library at home:** Reach out to the principal of your child's school and find out if you can get another set of school books to keep at home. For children experiencing ADHD, taking home the right books for assignments is challenging. So, having a backup set they can fall back on at home can be life-changing on the worst days.
- **Plan homework time:** Starting homework immediately after returning from school is a good habit much miss out on. Of course, it seems like no fun, especially after a whole day of learning. However, that is not half of it. Having a snack before plunging back into school work is advisable for some children. At the same time, their break could be some minutes of playtime or exercise.

If you try this break time after school, note how your child reacts. If they need the time to let off pent-up energy and regain their focus, it is a worthwhile addition to your schedule. First, create a designated homework area. It does not have to be anything fancy; your kitchen island, or the dining table, could suffice.

Alternatively, you could use your child's room. However, there are drawbacks to this option. For one, they are in their own space and may be more prone to distraction. Furthermore, it helps to be within reaching distance from them to answer questions and provide prompts as necessary. Moreover, since their bedrooms are often more isolated, this approach may not work correctly.

Some children prefer the quiet when doing homework, while others enjoy some background music at home. There are even children who prefer to work intermittently with little short breaks in between. Speak to your child and find out their preferred environment.

Finally, prioritize ease and predictability over sophistication in creating a homework routine. Once homework is completed, review it to ensure it has been done right. Then, help them put it away in their homework folder and return all the other items they use to their respective places.

STRATEGIES FOR ADHD CHILDREN AT SCHOOL

When pairing up with your child's teachers, it helps to give them some tips about engaging with your child. Doing so could make tutoring much more manageable while creating a safe space and structure for your child outside the home.

- **Be flexible with rules:** Children with ADHD often experience restlessness. So, while standard classrooms have rules about students staying in their seats for lessons, children with ADHD may struggle with this rule. Instead, they could focus better by standing or pacing. For the children who get fidgety, palming a tiny Koosh ball or something easy to maneuver in their hands helps with stimulation without causing disruptions. Some studies claim that chewing gum could even help boost the concentration of some students with ADHD. However, the research was pretty inconclusive. Furthermore, given how many schools frown on chewing gum, it is unlikely such changes may be allowed.
- **Acknowledge and reward positive behavior:** Incentives and rewards should always take center stage in motivating students instead of punishment and criticism. Changing rewards often could spice things up and create healthy competition to avoid boring the students. Children should not be prevented from going to recess as punishment for bad behavior.

Children with ADHD are, in fact, better able to focus after physical activity in a gym class or outdoors. In all, prioritizing rewards and incentives gives the school or classroom a favorable structure for children with ADHD.

- **Allow them some leeway:** Children with ADHD find it difficult to sit still for an extended period, so giving them room to leave their seats and move around the class could help them immensely. This subject should be handled cautiously so as not to disrupt the type or cause other students to want the same leeway.

Find creative ways to help them, like asking them to collect the notebooks of their peers, fetch materials from the storage closet, take a note to another official in the building, or wipe the board. Even something as minor as creating a little break time in between classes to let everyone get a drink of water at the fountain or from their lunch boxes helps a lot.

- **Encourage children to seek support:** children with ADHD require more help in class than other children, but it is unlikely that classroom aids are always available, in the same way, that academic support services for ADHD in schools may not be in place. So, while it could help for the child to be given a one-on-one audience with an adult, it is sometimes best to pair them up with their peers.

This pairing brings a child with ADHD into a group with another kind, mature classmate. The outcome is beneficial for both parties in terms of academics and socializing. For the child with ADHD, they have the chance to grow a relationship with their peers, improve their social skills, and show commitment. On the other hand, the study buddy makes a new friend, regularly reminds the student with ADHD about schoolwork, offers encouragement, and helps them stay grounded until a task is complete.

- **Maintain a consistent level of expectations:** The classroom engagement rules should be simple to understand and straight to the point. They should also be reviewed and updated regularly to stay abreast of changes. Rules should also be highlighted in an area of the classroom where they can be easily accessed.

It helps children read the rules and what is expected of them. This way, teachers can determine their understanding of it. Students can read the rules without understanding their meanings or implications.

For students who experience difficulty switching between tasks or lessons or managing time in general, having a schedule in hand and going over it regularly can ease them into the transition process better. Alternatively, you can use verbal cues, time signals, or timers to alert them of the duration of activity at any given time.

- **Give feedback regularly:** Both children with and without ADHD can benefit from regular feedback about their behaviors in class. In the same way, consequences for behavior, whether positive or negative, should also be meted out quickly.
- **Tone-down distractions:** Children with ADHD are often prone to distractions, so it could help to seat them away from potential sources of disruptions, such as windows, pencil sharpeners, doors, and cubby areas. Also, tone down the distractions in the classroom, including visual stimuli like clutter or sound stimuli like noise.

Putting on white noise or soft music to play in the background can help improve concentration and focus in children with ADHD. However, there is a tendency for it to be distracting for other children without the condition.

- **Avoid overloading them:** children with ADHD are easily prone to overwhelm. To counter such occurrences, consider breaking down the total workload into smaller bits for easier assimilation. Also, children are more likely to consider smaller micro-tasks easier to navigate than the same tasks lumped into one big whole.

Furthermore, children with ADHD may also experience sleep problems, which affects how much attention they pay in class and their overall behavior. Younger students are generally better prepared for learning earlier in the day when energy levels are high. However, you may experience a slump in productivity and energy after lunch. For older students, though, like teenagers and college students, morning classes are a chore.

That said, create a system that allows the class to handle more challenging and pressing subjects and schoolwork during the most engaged, alert, and productive periods.

In conclusion, remember that children with ADHD may struggle with attending school, staying focused in class, and doing after-school tasks like homework or projects. As a parent, show support by being compassionate about their struggles and helping to create a stable structure that eases the pressure on them. To do this, you need effective strategies that help your child improve at school and schoolwork while also imbibing necessary life skills. Finally, do not be afraid to reach out to the school and collaborate with teachers to create healthy and helpful structures for your child.

8

ADHD MEDICATION AND TREATMENT

ADHD can get frustrating to manage, especially at the onset of the diagnosis. In addition, you are usually torn between grief and anxiety, making the process all the more frustrating. However, you can take respite in the fact that there are prescription medications to help with the condition. While these drugs may not outrightly heal your child, they can help manage symptoms and give them a more normal life.

MEDS ON, MEDS OFF – WHEN AND WHEN NOT TO TAKE MEDICATION FOR ADHD

Usually, when your child requires ADHD medications, the signs are clear as day, with impairments in executive functions being the most prevalent symptoms. But how do you know these symptoms and tell them apart from youthful exuberance? Here are some signs to look out for:

- The child struggles at school and is often behind on schoolwork
- They find it challenging to develop and maintain friendships
- They exhibit behavioral problems both at home and at school
- They struggle with sports and after-school activities

ADHD medications—stimulants- typically—are the recommended treatment methods for children manifesting any of these signs because they address the core symptoms of the condition. Alternatively, you could take the path of behavioral therapy or combine it with the recommended stimulants.

When you are sure that their behavioral issues are more than childhood shenanigans and have got a diagnosis to back it up, you might want to start ADHD medications. But before you do, speak to the child and consult a medical professional.

Stopping Medications

Nevertheless, just as it is important to know when to start medicating, it is also crucial to know when to stop. Knowing when to stop medicating is not as clear-cut as knowing when to start, especially when the child is doing much better than beforehand. It makes you wonder if they should not continue the medication for life.

While it might seem like a reasonable proposition, there are a lot of other factors to consider. Here are some to take into cognizance during decision-making:

- Hesitation on your part, say, during the start of a new school year, to see how they fare without the medication
- Side effects. Many ADHD medications come with several adverse effects, including but not limited to moodiness, loss of appetite, or insomnia
- Children may begin rejecting medications, especially as they mature into teenagers

Although these reasons are not unfounded, they are not good enough to justify stopping ADHD medications. For instance, if the child is experiencing frequent side effects of the drugs, changing the medication or lowering the dose may bring better results than quitting altogether.

But another caveat is that many pediatricians and parents are skeptical about halting a good run of form and will likely keep the child on medication regularly without considering necessity. Nevertheless, whatever the case, you should continue to track your child's progress even after adjusting the dosage or changing medications.

When deciding to stop medicating, collaborate with your child's doctor to look for signs suggesting that moving past medications may be okay. That said, here are some reasons to consider:

- On days that the child is not on the medication, or when they fail to take it, symptoms are unnoticeable
- You had maintained the exact dosage over time, even when the child grew older and added a few pounds
- Your child has been doing well, with controlled behavior, and no symptoms of ADHD in the past year since beginning medication

TIPS FOR STOPPING ADHD MEDICATION AND MINIMIZING SIDE EFFECTS

Do not just quit the medication for the child. Instead, speak with the child and consult your doctor like when you started it. Then, let it be a unanimous decision to try stopping the medication.

Take cognizance of the possible risks of quitting ADHD medications and how they can affect the child. You want to ensure a safe transition for your child. For instance, non-stimulant meds like clonidine should not be stopped cold turkey. Doing so could lead to spikes in blood pressure. Professional medical guidance and oversight are needed for this process.

Time the process to coincide with low-stress periods of the year, such as when the child has adapted to school routines or after tests or exams. Waiting for holidays or vacations can also be a bad idea, as the child is not under the duress of schoolwork and might be less oversaturated. Instead, you want to find a time when everything is balanced and just a little easier.

After you stop medicating, schedule regular checkups at home and school to ensure that the child is still performing well, do not wait until the report card comes in to find out or for the teacher to ring you up. Instead, provide your child's teachers with a questionnaire to complete over several weeks, like the Vanderbilt Assessment Follow-Up form. There is also a form for parents, which should be forwarded with the teachers' form to your child's doctor. It is not up to their medical eye to decide if quitting the medication has been working fine for the child.

Compliance with ADHD Medication

Since stimulants like Adderall and Ritalin are widely abused and used outside the medical context, especially by teenagers and young adults, many parents do not imagine their child will have a problem taking ADHD medications. However, many children struggle with compliance as they enter teenagehood, whether they have taken the medications before or are just starting. This stems from their growing sense of independence, which makes them more likely to resist being medicated for chronic conditions.

Here are some tips to help win the compliance battle:

- Adjust the dosage or change the medication if the sole reason for noncompliance is side effects. You could even suggest lower symptoms in contrast to abandoning medicating altogether.
- Consult your child's doctor to find out if something else is going on with the child, like

oppositional defiant disorder, depression, substance use, and anxiety that may fuel their resistance.
- As in the beginning, get your child involved in the decision-making process. Instead of imposing it on them, try to find their reasons for noncompliance.
- Consider letting the child stop medicating during the weekends and other school breaks or holidays to see how they fare.
- Solicit help during and after school hours when switching ADHD medications to ensure your child is being monitored.
- Open a dialogue with your child and ensure they understand that the medication is neither a crutch nor a cure. It is like medicating for any other chronic condition, like how a person with insulin problems uses an EpiPen.

MEDICATION FOR TREATING ADHD

Stimulants

Stimulant medications are often prescribed to people with ADHD due to their effectiveness in improving symptoms of the condition. How it works is that the stimulants in the medication boost neurotransmitter levels in the brain. As such, the brain receives a shot of norepinephrine and dopamine, improving symptoms like hyperactivity, impulsivity, and inattention in people with ADHD.

Although stimulants are often the go-to medications for treating ADHD and are backed by the Food and Drug Administration (FDA) for use by children, many who use them do not respond to treatment or simply cannot tolerate stimulant therapy. There is also the case of people responding better to one form of stimulant over another.

When using stimulants, here are some of the most common side effects you can expect to experience: Irritability, dizziness, lower appetite, increased anxiety, and insomnia. Other side effects are not as widespread as those mentioned above, such as tics, blurry vision, mild stomach aches, increased heart rate and blood pressure, and nausea.

It helps to know and expect these side effects since they influence how willing you are to take or adhere to the medication. If your child experiences side effects from stimulant medications, consult your doctor. Do not leave anything to chance. This is so that you can safely quit or adjust the dosage of the medication under medical supervision.

The most common stimulant medications used for treating ADHD are Focalin (dexmethylphenidate), Adderall (amphetamine and dextroamphetamine), Dyanavel XR (amphetamine), Vyvanse (lisdexamfetamine), Daytrana or Concerta (methylphenidate), Zenzedi or Dexedrine (dextroamphetamine), Ritalin, Methylin, Metadate CD (methylphenidate), and Desoxyn (methamphetamine).

Non-Stimulants

Although stimulants are the typical first choice for many people treating ADHD, other non-stimulant medication options are also available. The entire premise of these medications is as follows:

- When stimulants cause too many side effects
- For people with a history of drug use
- When you do not respond to stimulants
- For people with a history of specific heart conditions
- For people with a history of bipolar disorder

Here are some non-stimulant medications you can use for your child:

- **Strattera:** Strattera (Atomoxetine) is one of the first medications outside of stimulants that the

FDA approved for treating attention deficit hyperactivity disorder in both adults and children above age six. Some potential side effects of this medication are vomiting, fatigue, agitation, irritability, dry mouth, decreased appetite, stomachache, increased blood pressure, dizziness, nausea, and increased heart rate.

- **Tricyclic antidepressants (TCAs):** Tricyclic antidepressants are not technically ADHD medications and are used off-label for treatment. Some of the commonly used drugs in this category are Tofranil (imipramine), Norpramin (desipramine), Amitriptyline, and Pamelor (nortriptyline). These drugs may cause side effects such as vivid dreams, drowsiness, dry mouth, insomnia, constipation, headaches, stomachache, and blurred vision.
- **Effexor:** Effexor (venlafaxine) is another off-label ADHD medication that is an antidepressant. It helps to improve mood and boost concentration. Common side effects of the drug include tremors, anxiety, nausea, sleep problems, dry mouth, and sexual problems in adults.
- **Wellbutrin:** Wellbutrin (bupropion) is another form of antidepressant medication. It has been

found to lower depression symptoms in many users and ADHD symptoms. However, some side effects of Wellbutrin include insomnia, irritability, worsening of existing tics, and weight loss caused by reduced appetite.
- **Anti-hypertensive drugs:** Other medications used for treating ADHD are heart blood pressure drugs, like Tenex (guanfacine) and Catapres (clonidine). They help to manage symptoms of ADHD but may cause side effects such as fatigue, stomach pain, decreased blood pressure, nausea, dry mouth, insomnia, dizziness, and drowsiness.

Of the non-stimulant medications mentioned in this section, Strattera is the most studied for use as ADHD treatment in children and adults. As a result, studies show fewer side effects when using it compared to others, like TCAs. Strattera is also more effective for ADHD than Wellbutrin.

Other Medications

Some people fail to respond to stimulant and non-stimulant medications or experience intolerable side effects. When that happens, medical professionals may offer other medications, such as guanfacine or clonidine, which the FDA approves for use by adolescents and children for managing ADHD symptoms. For people with no problems using stimulants, guanfacine or clonidine could also be administered to boost the effects of the medication.

Less common alternatives are often antidepressants like Wellbutrin (bupropion), although it is not FDA-approved for managing ADHD symptoms.

COPING WITH SIDE EFFECTS OF ADHD MEDICATION

Below are some common side effects of ADHD medication and how to treat them:

- **Headaches:** You can alleviate headaches in your child by administering the medication during or after mealtimes. However, there are times when headaches stem from deficiencies in vital minerals. This situation is noteworthy because some children with ADHD have magnesium deficiencies, which can lead to headaches.
- **Problems with sleeping:** Children with ADHD may face sleep problems regularly. Often, the medications they take may affect their ability to fall asleep. Other times, the restlessness symptom of ADHD comes into play, making it harder to go to sleep.

To combat this problem, you must set up a good sleep routine for your child. Make the time memorable for them, and put them in the mood for bedtime. Here are some helpful tips:

Start preparing them for sleep some 30 minutes before their bedtime. Although it may not be time to go to sleep, it helps to engage your child in quiet activities. For instance, switching from a fast-paced video game or sport to bedtime in minutes can cause sleeplessness. So, you want to steer the child towards activities like coloring, piecing together puzzles, or reading.

Work on their hygiene routine by encouraging them to use the bathroom, brush their teeth, wash their hands or take a bath, change into pajamas, turn off bright lights, and get into bed. Stick to this routine religiously, and try to get your child in and out of bed, as this will help you create a wake-up and bedtime routine.

- Reduced appetite: Feed your child healthy snacks rich with calories across the day. Some foods to try are:
- Toast and a hard-boiled egg
- Crackers and cheese
- A muffin served with a glass of milk
- A banana or apple served with peanut butter
- A protein bar

Consult your doctor for advice about administering medication after mealtimes.

- Stomach aches: Only administer medications during or after meals to reduce the likelihood of stomach problems.

CONTACTING THE DOCTOR

If these strategies discussed so far have failed to improve side effects in your child, consult your doctor immediately. In addition, seek advice on other side effects, such as tics (involuntary vocal or motor movements like throat clearing, muscle tensing, excessive eye blinking, coughing, or facial grimaces), irritability, and increased anxiety levels.

ADHD medications also have potential risks that you should discuss with the doctor. For example, non-stimulant medications like Qelbree (viloxazine) and Strattera (Atomoxetine) warn about triggering suicidal behaviors and thoughts. Therefore, you want to monitor your child using these medications to track changes in their behaviors or mood.

Do not fail to bring up potentially serious side effects and your child's medical history. These factors play a role in determining the best medication for the child and give you insights into what to consider when a situation arises.

PHARMACOGENETIC TESTING

Since ADHD is a complex condition, finding the best combination and volume of medications can be a chore. Depending on genetic makeup, some people metabolize medicines faster or slower than others. As a result, medications linger in the body for extended periods, leading to side effects. On the other hand, when they go through the body too quickly, their effectiveness wanes.

Thankfully, advances in technology and genetic testing provide people with ADHD with new knowledge about the type of medicine and the proper dosage to achieve the best results for treating the condition. In some instances, gene-based testing removes the need for trial and error, which is both expensive and frustrating.

Gene-based testing analyzes how medicines are metabolized in the body, showing the types of drugs that will give you the best results. This helps you avoid unpleasant side effects and guides the doctor in finding the proper dosage for your child. For example, many people who take amphetamines like Adderall suffer from nausea. A genetic test will show how your child's body reacts to this drug. With that knowledge, your doctor can begin lowering side effects through altered dosage or medications.

For instance, with a non-stimulant like Atomoxetine, the medication goes through the body faster. However, since some percentage of the population have a slower metabolism for such drugs, the Atomoxetine may linger in the body for 24 hours. This could make the treatment ineffective and trigger frequent side effects. Whatever type of medication you choose for your child, ensure that they are backed by a medical professional, including dosages. Having your child undergo gene-based testing before you begin medicating for the best results is also essential.

Although not everyone will love the process, it provides valuable information about well-being and treatment options crucial to lowering side effects and improving drug effectiveness.

9

NATURAL REMEDIES FOR TREATING ADHD

Although prescription medications are the way to treat attention deficit hyperactivity disorder, other natural remedies work well to reduce symptoms of the condition. For many, these natural remedies mean fewer side effects triggered by pharmaceutical concoctions. Natural remedies, also known as complementary and alternative medicines (CAM), typically revolve around lifestyle and dietary changes.

NATURAL STRATEGIES AND REMEDIES FOR TREATING ADHD

- **Sleep:** Helping your child nail down a good night routine is critical to quality sleep. Getting the recommended hours of shut-eye helps to reduce ADHD symptoms. For instance, if your child procrastinates on homework until the last minute, they may go to bed late. And that means little sleep, as their busy minds will keep them up longer than necessary. In turn, they will wake up groggy in the morning and still tired from not getting enough rest. ADHD affects your child's ability to concentrate or focus, and poor sleep only worsens that. If it continues, their mood and overall well-being will suffer, too.

- **Exercise:** Exercise helps with improvements in ADHD symptoms, mainly executive functions. Many studies have attempted to identify the different forms of exercise and their impact on ADHD. The final verdict is that all exercise types work just as well for the condition.

So, rather than focusing on type, the main objective should be to select an exercise routine your child enjoys. Ridiculous as it seems, enjoyment is a major driving factor in forming habits. Moreover, since a healthy habit like exercising helps with ADHD, it is worth cultivating. The workout routine does not have to be fancy; it could be simple exercises like martial arts, spinning classes, running, or yoga. To avoid boredom, you could even diversify the routine with multiple activities.

Some studies suggest that taking some time to enjoy the outdoors could help boost ADHD symptoms. Exercising can be an excellent way to combine physical activities and outdoor time.

- **Energetic play:** Exercise affects two significant symptoms of ADHD the most: impulsivity and hyperactivity. While children can have fun with organized physical activities like martial arts or sports, they may also benefit from energetic play several times a day. Active play can be anything from biking to playing on a trampoline, hopping with friends, or running around the yard with siblings.
- **Nutrition:** Diet is another aspect of your child's life affecting ADHD symptoms. Making conscious plans to feed them healthy foods, reduce junk food, and find food intolerances can help immensely.
- **Clean eating:** Some studies show that specific food additives and ingredients could exacerbate ADHD symptoms. For instance, sodium benzoate, found in many common drinks and foods, has been linked to some of the highest ADHD rating scales. Another is monosodium

glutamate, a flavor enhancer in many foods, such as baby food, bouillon cubes, and salad dressing. Some studies even report unhealthy cognitive reactions due to MSG.

Caffeine also enters the fray. As a stimulant, it worsens ADHD symptoms while improving dopamine flow, increasing alertness and focus. This complex trade-off results from side effects such as insomnia, nervousness, and anxiety. Caffeine is also known to impact stimulant medications negatively. There have also been studies linking additives and food coloring to hyperactivity symptoms in children.

- **Food intolerances:** Some studies suggest that people with ADHD are more likely to experience food intolerances and allergies than others. Common symptoms of intolerance are swelling of the tongue, hives, problems with breathing, or itchiness. A simple blood or skin test can diagnose your child with food allergies.

Food intolerances, on the other hand, are not so easy to diagnose. For instance, they may not be detected in blood tests, and the side effects of eating a specific food may not come immediately. However, intolerances gravely affect the quality of life. For instance, they can lead to decreased energy levels. They could also increase the likelihood of impulsiveness in your child and lower cognitive clarity or their ability to focus.

- **Protein:** Adding protein to your child's meal can help them to deal with symptoms of ADHD. Proteins have immense effects on neurotransmitters, like norepinephrine and dopamine, which are essential chemicals in managing ADHD symptoms. Neurotransmitters are biochemical communication links through which brain cells interact.

On the other hand, protein also helps to regulate blood sugar levels, which helps with brain function. Stimulant ADHD medications replicate these effects by boosting the flow of neurotransmitters in the brain's synapses. Therefore, having enough protein in their meals could help improve the function and efficiency of neurotransmitters. This could mean better performance for your child throughout the day. Therefore, making an ADHD meal for your child should consist of a decent balance of fiber and protein sourced from oatmeal, unprocessed fruit, and vegetables.

- **Blood sugar:** Although the study on the link between ADHD symptoms and high-sugar dietary patterns was somewhat inconclusive, some evidence shows that diets rich in sugar may worsen specific ADHD symptoms. If your child overeats sugar, the glucose level in their blood will fluctuate, and they may experience energy crashes. These changes can exacerbate ADHD symptoms in focus, memory, and activity levels.

Rather than encouraging your child to eat unhealthy snacks and junk food, turn their attention to foods rich in fiber and protein. Go for snacks loaded with these natural ingredients to leave them feeling fuller for extended periods. Protein and fiber also help to regulate the movement of blood sugar levels.

- **Elimination diet:** An elimination diet can be done in two main ways. For one, you can remove the top causes of allergies from your child's meal, including chocolate, eggs, dairy, soy, peanuts, corn, shellfish, wheat, and yeast. Alternatively, you could take them out one by one and track whether or not your child's symptoms reduce.

The first method is likely unadvisable because taking out so many foods from your child's diet grossly reduces their options. Instead, they end up with a restrictive diet, which is challenging to keep up with. There is also the likelihood that your child will suffer from nutritional deficiencies. Therefore, the best way to begin eliminating foods from their diet is to consult a dietician. This way, you have medical professionals offering guidance on how to proceed.

BEHAVIORAL THERAPY AND ADHD

Behavioral therapy is an umbrella term for types of therapy that treat mental health disorders. This therapy seeks to identify and help change potentially self-destructive or unhealthy behaviors. It functions on the idea that all behaviors are learned and that unhealthy behavior can be changed. Therefore, the focus of treatment is often on current problems and how to change them.

Types of Behavioral Therapy

There are many different types of behavioral therapy:

▷ **Aversion Therapy**

Aversion therapy is often used to treat substance abuse and alcoholism problems. It works by teaching people to associate a desirable but unhealthy stimulus with a highly unpleasant one. The unpleasant stimulus may be something that causes discomfort. For example, a therapist may teach you to associate alcohol with an unpleasant memory.

▷ **Cognitive Behavioral Play Therapy**

Cognitive behavioral play therapy is commonly used with children. By watching children play, therapists can gain insight into what a child is uncomfortable expressing or unable to express. For example, children may be able to choose their toys and play freely. They might be asked to draw pictures or use toys to create scenes in a sandbox. Therapists may teach parents how to use play to improve communication with their children.

▷ **System Desensitization**

System desensitization relies heavily on classical conditioning. It is often used to treat phobias. People are taught to replace a fear response to a phobia with relaxation responses. A person is first taught relaxation and breathing techniques. Once mastered, the therapist will slowly expose them to their fear in heightened doses while they practice these techniques.

▷ **Cognitive Behavioral Therapy**

Cognitive behavioral therapy is viral. It combines behavioral therapy with cognitive therapy. Treatment is centered around how someone's thoughts and beliefs influence their actions and moods. It often focuses on a person's current problems and how to solve them. The long-term goal is to change a person's thinking and behavioral patterns to healthier ones.

BEHAVIORAL THERAPY FOR CHILDREN WITH ADHD

Applied behavior therapy and play therapy are both used for children. Treatment involves teaching children different methods of responding to situations more positively.

A central part of this therapy is rewarding positive behavior and punishing negative behavior. Parents must help to reinforce this in the child's day-to-day life. It may take children some time to trust their counselor; this is normal. However, they will eventually warm up to them if they feel they can express themselves without consequences. Children with autism and ADHD often benefit from behavioral therapy.

BEHAVIORAL THERAPIST - WHY YOU NEED ONE AND HOW TO GET ONE

Finding a therapist can feel overwhelming, but many resources make it easier. When finding a provider, you can choose from:

- Social workers
- Faith-based counselors
- Non-faith-based counselors
- Psychologists
- Psychiatrists

You should ensure that your chosen provider has the necessary certifications and degrees. Some providers will focus on treating specific conditions, such as eating disorders or depression.

If you do not know how to get started finding a therapist, you can ask your doctor for a recommendation. They may recommend you to a psychiatrist if they think you might benefit, as psychiatrists can write prescriptions for medication.

Most insurance plans will cover therapy. Some providers offer scholarships or sliding-scale payments for low-income individuals. A therapist will ask you many personal questions about yourself. You will know you have found the right therapist if you feel comfortable talking to them. You may have to meet with several therapists to find the right one.

In conclusion, prescription drugs are the obvious way to treat a condition like ADHD. However, they are not always good as they have side effects that may be much more severe in different people.

Thankfully, some natural remedies and therapies have proved quite effective in treating ADHD. You can get in touch with a qualified professional who will be able to guide you more on the therapies and bring in better results.

Luckily, you do not need professional support for using natural remedies, as it is doubtful they have any adverse effects.

10

SUPPORT RESOURCES FOR PARENTS

Given a choice, many parents would not choose to raise children with ADHD. Not because the children are a curse to be shunned, but due to the sheer effort that goes into it. But over the years, the pressure of raising children with the condition has lessened thanks to increased awareness and improvements in treatment methods. ADHD is no longer the dreaded and misunderstood condition it once was.

With the myriad of help available, you just have to find the right resources to help you cope in your journey to provide your child with a normal life.

BEST ADHD PODCASTS

- **The Faster Than Normal Podcast**: This podcast relays the success stories of people living with ADHD. From CEOs to rock stars to everyday people, guests come on to speak about finding success in work and day-to-day life, regardless of their condition. This podcast might be the pick-me-up you need to change your mindset about how you see ADHD and its impact on your child's future.
- **I Have ADHD**: Kristen Carder, an ADHD life coach, hosts this podcast. She dedicates the show to teaching people with ADHD vital organizational and time management skills. Listen to this podcast daily if you need practical tips to help your child set goals and be productive.
- **CHADD**: CHADD is an acronym for Children and Adults with Attention Deficit Disorder. The organization was created in 1987 to create awareness for people with ADHD. CHADD is a network of volunteers who help to teach, encourage, and support people living with ADHD, including teachers and parents.
- **Distracted**: Mark Patey is the founder of this podcast. He was in fifth grade when his

diagnosis turned up as ADHD. Afterward, he was placed in a special education class with children considered troublemakers and others with severe disabilities. Regardless of the difficulties ADHD created for him, Mark grew up to become a businessman. And a successful one, too. On Distracted, he talks about what the diagnosis means and how it should not be the trigger for a negative spiral.

- **ADHD reWired**: Eric Tivers, founder of ADHD reWired, is a coach, therapist, and Licensed Clinical Social Worker (LCSW). His approach to the podcast is different from most on this list. He does not just bring on experts on the condition; he also reaches out to regular folks living with ADHD. His listeners benefit from listening to relatable stories from relatable people and hearing actionable strategies from experts.
- **Adult Attention Deficit Disorders Center of Maryland**: This podcast is a collaborative platform shared by Valerie L. Goodman, a clinical psychotherapist and LCSW-C, and David W. Goodman, a medical doctor, and professor of psychiatry and behavioral sciences. The duo offers various resources, from practical to educational, for helping people with

ADHD. Their audio interviews and podcasts aim to tackle common problems encountered by people with the condition, like being diagnosed with another mental health issue besides ADHD.

- **Parenting ADHD**: Penny Williams hosts the Parenting ADHD podcast. She is a mom who took it upon herself to find out every last detail about ADHD when her son was diagnosed. This is the closest relatable podcast of the lot. So, you can start from here, if you would like. Penny is now a coach and author who partners with parents to teach them about their children's condition. Her podcast has several episodes that discuss all the necessary details on parenting ADHD children, including relaxing activities, homework, and positive parenting.
- **ADHD Experts**: On this podcast, high-profile experts on ADHD are brought in to help discuss issues on work life, family life, and education. Unlike other podcasts on this list, ADHD Experts uses a more interactive format. Questions are collected from parents with ADHD children and adults living with the condition. To participate in the show, simply register for the live webinar.

- **More Attention, Less Deficit**: Ari Tuckman, the host of this podcast, is a psychologist, MBA, and PsyD, who prioritizes the diagnosis and treatment of adults, teenagers, and children living with ADHD, including other related conditions. He wrote a book titled "More Attention, Less Deficit" to aid adults with attention deficit hyperactivity disorder. He goes over various issues per episode on the podcast, providing practical steps to creating positive changes.
- **ADHD Support Talk Radio**: Tara McGillicuddy is an ADHD expert and the creator and director of ADDClasses.com. Her podcast focuses on important challenges and problems people with ADHD experience. She pairs up with other experts to discuss several issues on ADHD, including future planning, stress management, and financial management, among other things.
- **Practical ADHD Strategies**: Laura Rolands was a human resource professional with over 15 years of experience. In 2009, she became an ADHD coach and created MyAttentionCoach.com. In this podcast, Laura shares some great tips for managing the condition. She also conducts interviews with

experts in fields like mindfulness and time management.

- **Adulting with ADHD**: This podcast is designed for a specific audience: Women. Sarah Snyder, the host, goes over personal stories of her experiences with the condition. Other times, she brings on other women with ADHD to talk about relevant subjects such as menopause, pregnancy, and postpartum depression.
- **Taking Control: The ADHD Podcast**: This podcast was created by Nikki Kinzer, PCC and certified ADHD coach. She helps her listeners develop helpful strategies for dealing with stress, improving productivity levels, organizing, and managing time. On the show, Kinzer looks at some of the specific areas in which people with ADHD find trouble. Afterward, she provides practical tips for solving the problems.

BEST ADHD APPS

When picking an app for your child with ADHD, consider its ease of use, its vital features, and its availability on Android and iOS. The apps highlighted in the section are selected for their high ratings and glowing reviews, ensuring that they were used by actual people and worked as intended. This way, you can get good value for your resources.

Some of the best ADHD apps are Bear, Evernote, Asana, Due – Reminders and Timers, Trello, Remember the Milk, Clear Todos, Brain Focus, Simple-Mind Pro – Mind Mapping, Todoist, and Productive – Habit Tracker.

Facebook Support Groups

Facebook is easily one of the largest social media networks for connecting with communities that matter to you. From groups to pages, there is something for everyone, including people with ADHD or parents of ADHD children.

Joining one of these groups may seem daunting, as you do not know anyone there. But do not despair; everyone in such a group is united under the banner of ADHD. The community is vital because it makes the condition relatable and much easier to deal with now that it is clear you are not alone.

Here are some of the reasons to join a Facebook group about ADHD and what you stand to gain:

- **Vent:** Dealing with ADHD is so challenging that parents battle depression, anxiety, or OCD when caring for their children. Facebook groups allow you to vent about your challenges each day and get the frustration off your chest, knowing fully well that you are surrounded by folks who understand.

- **Ask questions:** Pose questions to people with ADHD and parents with children with a similar condition. Ask them if they forget to do their hair before driving the children to school or if they fell asleep at work from overworking the previous day. Ask everything and anything.

Consider joining Parent Support Group for ADHD/ODD and Autistic children. Alternatively, you could just enter "ADHD" into any old search engine and find groups or pages that work for you.

In conclusion, whether you need some strong tips to deal with the condition or want to know more about ADHD for the sake of your child, using any of the support or resources discussed in this chapter can help greatly. Your child can live a normal life with hopes for future success.

11

MAKING AND KEEPING FRIENDS

Making friends is a big deal for children. Although children experience trouble making and keeping friends, the social difficulties children with ADHD face must be expertly managed. Children with ADHD struggle more with building friendships for many reasons connected to their ADHD symptoms. The symptoms of ADHD make proper engagement with others a herculean task for the child, causing frustration. Although parents would love to address the bad behavior resulting from that frustration, addressing the root cause is better.

Making and maintaining friendships requires tons of skills like talking, sharing, listening, and being empathetic, which children with ADHD do not acquire naturally. As a parent, this can be a constant source of worry. Children with ADHD cannot pick up social skills that other children assimilate at a higher rate. Because their symptoms make them neglect social cues, children with ADHD potentially drive others away from them.

Before a child is diagnosed with ADHD, the social isolation from other children can be unexplainable and worrisome, as it seems the ADHD child has a wrong air around them, which other children seem to avoid. They may attend a few playdates but never get invited back.

When children are much younger, it is difficult to detect their lack of social skills because other children might only wonder why they display such an attitude but might not take offense. Again, when children are much younger, their playdates have the presence of a parent or caregiver. But the lack of social skills becomes much more noticeable as the child grows, causing alienation during playtime because now other children can take offense.

Children with ADHD need help to learn how to build and maintain friendships. The bulk of the work lies on parents, who have to make this work without upsetting their children. If your ADHD child struggles with making friends, you have a lot of work cut out for you.

HELPING YOUR ADHD CHILD WITH BUILDING FRIENDSHIPS

- **Guide your child to overcome impulsivity:** Children with ADHD can not effectively control their impulses. They often interrupt their friends or have difficulty keeping up with the conversation flow. When this happens, their friends can become frustrated and may leave them behind or ignore them.

Although it will take time, regular practice will help your child interact better with others. Introducing children with ADHD to yoga or meditation can help them weigh their actions and initiate the best response. If the child is not old enough for yoga, getting them to sit still may be hard, but you can convert mindfulness into a game to help them practice.

Teach your child to pause and think about their options before deciding. Then, help them determine which choice will provide a positive response. When your child learns this at home, they will replicate it in their relationship with friends.

- **Guide your child to stop hitting:** When a child cannot control their impulse, their conversations with friends might not be the only thing affected. The impulsivity may make the children with ADHD hit others due to their anger and frustration. You can help them stop this act by determining exactly why it happens.

Usually, children react when they are put in a position they want to end. For example, they will react if your child's friend takes their toy or calls them a name. The best way to address this issue is to consider why the action happened—solving the why will prevent your child from hitting.

Children with ADHD should be shown ways to cope with anger and frustration, and exemplary action is the best way to do that. Whenever you negatively show anger to your child or partner, offer an apology.

This helps your child learn. Guide your child through ways to avoid confrontation, for instance, taking short, calming walks or taking several deep breaths. Children with ADHD are impulsive, so your child needs to learn to channel their impulses into other activities, like jumping jacks or running, until they are calm.

- **Guide your child to stop using rude words:** Parents of children with ADHD understand and excuse some of their children's behaviors because of their condition. However, if these children say rude or hurtful things, other children can label them as mean or bullies. As a parent, you can prevent name-calling when they use rude words by teaching your ADHD child empathy.

An angry response whenever your child uses rude language, will only escalate the situation. The best way to react to this will be to let them know how you felt about their comment. Doing this helps the child to understand that words can be impactful, helping the child be conscious and empathetic to others.

This same strategy can be applied when your child is rude to their friends. It will help them understand that their rude words were hurtful and initiate the process of mending the relationship. Most importantly, understand that your child cannot learn all these instantly, which will take quite a long time. Therefore, you have to apply patience as you help your child practice.

- **Helping your child to keep friends:** Children are likelier to keep friends when they have frequent playdates. A child of school age can develop socialization skills and build friendships if they interact with others outside of school. ADHD children benefit from playdates because you can make the environment safe for them to practice positive skills. The following tips will help you guide them to maintain friendships.

- **Teach your child to resolve conflicts:** During playtime, it is normal for children to have conflicts. However, conflicts are more frequent for children with ADHD due to impulsivity. When conflicts occur, teach your child that their actions can hurt their friends. A good way to make children with ADHD remorseful is to let them step into the shoes of the offended. Ask them how they would feel if they were in their friend's position. Then, ask them how they will want their friend to apologize. Get them to say or do those things to their friends to fix the conflict and rebuild the friendship.

- **Teach your child to prevent future conflicts:** It might take a while before you can get your ADHD child to avoid future conflict. However, you must ensure there is constant improvement. When there is a conflict, let your child practice resolution skills. Constant practice improves their confidence.

Ensure you remind your child to continue practicing "stop and think" skills so they can become an automatic part of your child's instincts. Then, as time goes on, they will impulsively stop, think, and respond instead of reacting.

- **Teach your child to avoid triggering situations:** Your child can maintain friendships by learning to stop triggering situations. While teaching your child how to manage their social skills and control their impulses, teach them, as well, to keep off from environments that cause conflicts.

When playing, they can avoid activities like roughhousing on the playground or at birthday parties. Although keep in mind that getting them off activities like this will help them manage their reactions, you should not restrict them from these activities forever. When the child's impulse control improves, allow them to use their "stop and think" skills to understand and predict situations that can trigger a physical conflict.

With increasing confidence levels, children with ADHD can understand their emotions and how they affect their interactions. Eventually, they will learn signs that show a situation will cause conflict and learn to steer clear before their impulse takes over.

- **How to achieve a successful playdate:** Having established that playdates are great for children to make friends, you need to have a plan to make it work. First, invite a playmate to whom your child is close. Ensure that the playmate has things in common with your child. Without shared interests, it will be difficult to have a successful date. Before the date, it is better to filter play activities to remove physical activities requiring high energy or physical contact. For instance, you can remove touch football from the playlist if your child cannot stop touching others.

TIPS TO HELP YOU PREPARE YOUR ADHD CHILD FOR A PLAYDATE

- **The guest gets to choose:** Let your child learn to step back for their guests. When a child visits, let your child know that a friend is welcome in the house as a guest while they play host. Although your child can suggest activities for playtime, the final decision lies with the guest.
- **Accept the guest completely:** Help your child remember not to criticize if they dislike their

friend's method of doing things because everyone has a different pattern.

- **Be kind to the guest:** Avoid inviting more than one friend at a time. Even though your child might know many other children, the others may not know or be friends. This could spark conflicts, putting your child in a position they cannot handle.
- **Avoid hovering, but be alert for intervention:** As long as you have taught your child good social skills, trust that they will use them. Encouraging your child to use healthy skills is a good way to reinforce them. It is good to be nearby but stay in another room so you can observe your child's reactions to potential conflict.

You cannot wholly erase disagreements from children's playdates. Instead, it would be best if you strived to help your child react better when they happen.

EXPLAINING YOUR CHILD'S ADHD BEHAVIOR TO OTHER PARENTS

One of the most challenging aspects of parenting a child with ADHD is explaining your child's behavior to other parents. For example, you probably have had to explain every time your child hit a friend or said rude things to them.

Many times, children with ADHD lose friends because other parents do not want their children to interact with them. This can cause pain for you and your child and fuel a continuous cycle of making and losing friends. Instead of watching your child grow lonely from not having friends, try to explain ADHD behaviors to other parents as much as possible. The following tips can help you:

- **Do not wait until a conflict happens:** Talk to the parents of your child's friend before any incident happens. Make them understand your child's behavior and let them know how you address it. This way, the other parents can handle your child's emotions without prejudice, and you can make them your allies in making a better life for your child.
- **Actively resolve conflict:** When there is a conflict, make an effort to resolve it to prevent escalation. Step aside with your child and discuss their behavior. Offer encouragement for the things that were done well and share ways to improve them in the future.
- **Reach out after a conflict:** Address the conflict when the parent of the offended child arrives

and ensure they know it has been resolved. Share the steps you took to achieve resolution. Listen to the other parent, so they know their concern about protecting their child is valid. This helps everyone part on a good note.

However, you must remember that even though everything is done right, parents may want to avoid future playdates. Let your child know that they do not have to be discouraged if this happens.

Most importantly, you and your child must understand that childhood friendships are fickle. They change often, and your child's friends will change while improving social skills. Help your child build self-awareness by discussing the playdates and determining which friend they would like to see more frequently. Monitor your child's behavior during playdates and use it as a learning experience. Do not send them to a friend's house for a playdate until conflict management skills are built. Helping a child with ADHD develop their social and friendship skills might be tasking, but it helps them have a better quality of life.

CONCLUSION

The reaction of many parents upon learning that their children have Attention Deficit Hyperactivity Disorder may range from despair, and anger, to apathy. In fact, some parents do not bother to learn why their children behave differently than others. You, who have made it to the end of this book, do not fall into either of those categories. Instead, you are not only eager to learn about your child's diagnosis but are also committed to finding the correct ways to parent your ADHD child. This is certainly commendable.

This book must have impressed you that ADHD is not a curse, if nothing else. This condition need not determine your child's future. Instead, they can attain greatness in whichever area of life interests them.

CONCLUSION

The first chapter of this book undertook the job of demystifying ADHD. The prevailing reason why people think this condition is unmanageable is ignorance. If such parents know anything about the condition, that knowledge most likely comes from unreliable sources. This book has strived to be empathetic because, without a doubt, ADHD can be challenging to deal with. But it also explained, in great detail, what the condition is.

For instance, Chapter One revealed the three types of ADHD. Your child who has this condition may either be hyperactive and impulsive, or they could be inattentive. The third type is a combination of inattentiveness and hyperactivity. As such, you should be careful not to assume that your child is incapable of or has difficulty paying attention simply because of their proclivity to be hyperactive.

Chapter Two continued from where the preceding chapter left off. It dispelled the myths and stated the facts regarding the causes of ADHD. Although genes, alcohol and substance abuse, and poor nutrition have been linked to ADHD, there is no proof that video games, TV, sugar consumption, and gender are causal factors of this condition. Unfortunately, some people still believe that girls cannot have this disorder, and misconceptions like that can be especially dangerous. It

CONCLUSION | 185

may lead to depression and suicidal ideation for girls whose claims are disregarded.

The third chapter of this book took us into the brains of people with ADHD. We learned, in this chapter, how the brains of people with this disorder differ from those of neurotypicals. This book section was important as it conclusively did away with the notion that ADHD may only exist in the imagination of those diagnosed with it.

With the necessary foundational knowledge of ADHD carefully described, the succeeding chapters of this book, ***Parenting a Child with ADHD***, focus on solutions for parents with children with the disorder. From learning how to talk to your child with ADHD to effective parenting strategies, this book equipped you with the skills to provide adequate care for your child living with this disorder.

Nothing truly is worse than feeling guilty for being unable to help your child when you are certain they need it. And ADHD, especially for parents dealing with the disorder for the first time, can feel like a hopeless situation. But, thankfully, hope *does* exist.

This book is packed with carefully researched solutions and true and relatable anecdotes that'll guide you from despair to triumph. If you apply the knowledge in this book, your child will become more sociable, successful, and confident. Feel free to highlight the points in this book that you found important. Then, go back and reread what stuck out to you, and make notes or set reminders to enable you to consistently practice the solutions shared in this book.

Do not feel discouraged or disheartened if some solutions fail to produce the desired results quickly. If your will is strong and you are determined to help your child shine in ways you know they can, this book will surely work for you.

Parenting is a grueling job, and it is even tougher when ADHD is thrown into the mix. However, with the right resources, like this book, you will find that raising a great child into a stellar adult can be fun.

A Shining Opportunity to Help Another Parent

You're doing a remarkable thing, and everything you've learned here will make your journey that little bit easier. Now you have the perfect opportunity to give that chance to other parents!

Simply by leaving your honest opinion of this book on Amazon, you'll show new readers where they can find the guidance they're looking for - no matter how little time they have.

Thank you for your support. The parenting journey can feel terribly isolating at times - but when we share information, we see that none of us is really alone.

This is the beginning of your exciting journey with your child! If you'd like more awesome content and support from other parents just like you, then I invite you to join the

Parenting A Child With ADHD Facebook Community here:

REFERENCES

Cherry, K. (2021). What are the benefits of having ADHD?. Verywell Mind. https://www.verywellmind.com/adhd-benefits-advantages-challenges-and-tips-5199254

Dvorsky, M. R., & Langberg, J. M. (2016). A review of factors that promote resilience in youth with ADHD and ADHD symptoms. *Clinical Child and Family Psychology Review, 19(4)*, 368–391. https://doi.org/10.1007/s10567-016-0216-z

McBee, M. T., Brand, R. J., & Dixon, W. E. (2021). Challenging the link between early childhood television exposure and later attention problems: a multiverse approach. *Psychological Science, 32(4)*, 496–518. https://doi.org/10.1177/0956797620971650

Sherrell, Z. (2021). *6 strengths and benefits of ADHD*. Medical News Today. https://www.medicalnewstoday.com/articles/adhd-benefits

Swanson, J. M., Sunohara, G. A., Kennedy, J. L., Regino, R., Fineberg, E., Wigal, T., Lerner, M., Williams, L., LaHoste, G. J., & Wigal, S. (1998). Association of the dopamine receptor D4 (DRD4) gene with a refined phenotype of attention deficit hyperactivity disorder (ADHD): a family-based approach. *Molecular Psychiatry, 3(1)*, 38–41. https://doi.org/10.1038/sj.mp.4000354

Tovo-Rodrigues, L., Rohde, L. A., Menezes, A. M., Polanczyk, G. V., Kieling, C., Genro, J. P., Anselmi, L., & Hutz, M. H. (2013). DRD4 rare variants in Attention-Deficit/Hyperactivity Disorder (ADHD): further evidence from a birth cohort study. *PloS one, 8(12)*, e85164. https://doi.org/10.1371/journal.pone.0085164

Ulrich R. S. (1984). View through a window may influence recovery from surgery. *Science (New York, N.Y.), 224(4647)*, 420–421. https://doi.org/10.1126/science.6143402

www.ingramcontent.com/pod-product-compliance
Lightning Source LLC
Chambersburg PA
CBHW020310010526
44107CB00001B/52